The Relationship Between

# Government

# Economics

# And

# Freedom!

# The Relationship Between

# Government

# Economics

# And

# Freedom!

Kariem Abdul Haqq

**To order additional copies of this book, contact:**
Xlibris
844-714-8691
www.Xlibris.com
Orders@Xlibris.com
848188

The 13th Amendment Freedom Week Movement falls under The Freedom and Economic Education, Inc, which is a non-profit educational organization under the guidelines of the Internal Revenue Service Code 501C3, with tax-exempt status.

The ideals, principles, and aspirations of freedom, justice, and equal opportunity are promoted in the Movement. The 13th Amendment Freedom Week Movement was founded to establish an annual freedom celebration for the first time in American history when all law-abiding Americans were free, consequently ending chattel slavery.

This celebration is based upon the ratification of the 13th Amendment to the Constitution of the United States, December 6, 1865. It seeks the participation of all Americans regardless of race, religion, or creed. Its motto is to "Celebrate while you Educate!"

Website: www.13thamendmentfreedomweek.com

*"…I feel and seek The light I cannot see!"*

Samuel T. Coleridge


**"I had six honest serving men. They taught me
all I knew. Their names were Where and What
and When – And Why and How and Who."**

Rudyard Kipling

# Table of Contents

This book is dedicated to all freedom lovers and freedom fighters—past, present, and future.

Special acknowledgment is due to some exceptional men for their commitment and dedication to the struggle for freedom, justice, and equal opportunity (under the limited rule of law and free enterprise economics).

First among giants in the field of government is Frederic Bastiat, the Frenchman who gave us a small but super powerful book called ***THE LAW.*** It is a precious classic and a book that should be in every home, everywhere. To add substance and strength to this present book, the author has taken the liberty to interlace it with many quotes from Frederic Bastiat's own works.

Then there are Robert Welch and John F. McManus. Robert Welch gave us the little ***Blue Book***, and John F. McManus gave us the filmstrip, ***An Overview of our World*** (accompanied by its text in book form). Mr. McManus's filmstrip and the book about the five forms of government and the five types of economic systems, which the author saw and read many decades ago, had a major impact on his life. They have stuck in his mind ever since the first viewing and reading and are the foundation of this book.

When this author was trying to find his way, he went down many roads back in the day. Many were dead-end streets. In his late teens, he got involved in the Civil Rights Movement. It led him from a protest mentality to a revolutionary state of mind. Right in the heart of the American ghetto, he found himself reading the little ***Red Book*** by Mao Tse-tung, the **little *Black Book*** by Kwame Nkrumah, the **little *Green Book*** by Muammar Gaddafi, the Communist Manifesto, and a lot of other socialist's literature.

Dedication

While expressing his sympathies for the Marxist revolutionary ideology, this author was given another little book titled, ***None Dare Call It Conspiracy*** by Gary Allen. It opened his eyes and challenged his way of thinking to the point that he sought other books to gain more knowledge and understanding.

So when the little ***Blue Book*** by Robert Welch was presented to him, it would have shown a lack of sincerity, integrity, and courage for him not to read it, especially if objectivity and truth were what he was truly seeking.

The previous books dealing with socialism and revolutionary false data represented one extreme, and the little ***Blue Book*** represented the other. It was exactly what this author needed to balance his thinking and cross-check the information he had been receiving from many other nefarious sources. It proved to be the nemesis for his previous orientation toward communist and socialist propaganda and rhetoric, as well as the antidote needed for his previously chosen path of miseducation, lies, and deception.

Another great scholar and freedom fighter that the author wishes to recognize is the legendary Leonard E. Read, founder of the Foundation for Economic Education, Inc. (FEE). Through his great effort to organize an educational system that would teach those who had an undying love for the freedom philosophy and thirst and hunger for the truth, his name and fame should live in the hearts of all who love freedom, justice, and equal opportunity. He had a great and positive influence by introducing many to men like Frederic Bastiat, Ludwig Von Mises, Henry Hazlitt, Friedrich A. Hayek, G. Henry Weaver, etc. These men, along with him, authored many great books (precious gems) on ***the relationship between government, economics, and freedom.***

Last but not least among the giants in the field of Economics was Merrill Jenkins Sr. He was the founder of the Monetary Realist Society out of St. Louis, Missouri. Mr. Jenkins gave the world the greatest book on economics that the author has ever read, ***Money,*** *the Greatest Hoax on Earth.* He will always be dearly loved and profoundly missed by him and those who were fortunate enough to be by his side. This author would like to also take the privilege and honor to say that Merrill Jenkins Sr. was his personal friend and mentor.

Merrill's book is, for the most part, based upon accumulated knowledge. He stood on the shoulders of many great historical scholars of economics who came before him. However, he was able to see with an extraordinary feat of analytical power, something that others missed. And that something was the true meanings, natures, and functions of "money" and "interest" and their destructive effects on humanity as a whole. With that understanding, he was able to reform the entire subject of economics.

Merrill Jenkins Sr. was a genius. When it came to economics, his mind was penetrating, his focus was singular, and he did not back down from speaking the truth and delivering the facts to anyone. If a person wants to have the best understanding of economics, then *Money the Greatest Hoax on Earth* by Merrill Jenkins Sr. is the path to take.

Freedom is not a system. But the right 'system' (or form) of government and the right 'system' of economics contribute very much to the reality of freedom.

The heart and soul of *The Relationship between Government, Economics, and Freedom* are drawn, one way or another, from these men of genius. Their research and hard work laid the foundation for this book. And for that, the author is honored to give thanks and show gratitude for their role in helping him with a better understanding of the nature and the proper role of government, a clearer knowledge of economics (and "money" and "interest"), and their relationship to freedom. May God reward them for their good and for their contributions to those of us who are seekers of the truth.

Leonard E. Read, Founder of FEE stated it this way: *"Seekers after Truth should not be bound by who sponsors any idea – Truth being its own witness…. there is no place for idolatry in the freedom philosophy."* With that in mind, the author only asks one to carefully read this book, compare, and verify the information.

> *"The state is that great fiction by which everyone tries to live at the expense of everyone else."*
>
> Frederic Bastiat, "The Law"

Understanding the correlation between good government and good economics in terms of their effects on freedom, justice, and equal opportunity can abundantly benefit any individual, community, or nation.

*"Logical thinking and real life are not two separate orbits. Logic is for man the only means to master the problems of reality. What is contradictory in theory, is no less contradictory in reality. No ideological inconsistency can provide a satisfactory, i.e. working, solution for the problems offered by the facts of the world."*

This book will take complex human relationships and break them down into basic and simple logic that any common man or woman reader can easily understand.

It will provide an overview of the relationship between good government, sound economics, and freedom that can withstand the history of civilizations from the beginning of human existence through the ages.

The truth will set people free, but lies will keep them in bondage. This book will enlighten those who seek to understand causes and do not start and stop only at the effects. Shakespeare (Hamlet) stated it this way: *"And now remains that we find out the cause of this effect; or, rather say, the cause of this defect, for this effect defective comes by cause."*

This book is for those who believe in and seek truth and freedom. For, *"what cannot be found in human freedom cannot be truth."* It is for those who seek to understand the laws of God, the natural laws of the universe, and the laws of human nature and to build their government *forms* and economic systems in alignment with them.

They are the ones who pursue knowledge, wisdom, and justice…**and they leave no stones unturned!**

It is a book for the new and up-and-coming future leadership – Thinkers! Visionaries! The Patiently Consistent!

# Introduction

*"The solution to the problems of
human relationships is to be found in liberty."*

*Frederic Bastiat, "The Law"*

Mankind studies religion! Mankind studies politics! Mankind studies economics! Mankind explores all sorts of disciplines! But the common denominator that makes all of them succeed is Freedom!

Religion is man's relationship to his Creator (worship that leads to survival and salvation). Law (Justice, government, and politics) is man's relationship with man. And economics is man's relationship to the land (natural resources).

It is essential that mankind have spiritual, political, and economic freedoms to advance. All three areas of discipline are vast in scope and depth. They also interact with each other and overlap one another in many ways.

Each can take years of study alone for one to become an expert. It is even more challenging to integrate all three without losing either of their respective truths and principles.

There are five major religions in the world: Hinduism, Buddhism, Judaism, Christianity, and Islam. Most of the world's population professes one of these five world religions.

There are five basic *forms* of government that can exist or have ever existed throughout the history of humanity. They are Monarchy, Oligarchy, Democracy, Republic, and Anarchy.

And there are three types of economic systems that have existed throughout history. These three include:

1.  Free Market Economics (commonly known as capitalism)

2.  Socialism with its many shades (Feudalism, Mercantilism, Fascism, Nazism, mixed economy)

3.  Communism (which can never get past the stage of socialism)

The last two are a combination of government and so-called legislated planned "economics."

This book will not focus on religion, which is man's relationship to his Creator. Any of the five religions can be compatible with good government and good economics if the people of those respective religions have the understanding, wisdom, and desire to bring good "limited" government and good "free enterprise" economics in harmony with their faith.

Religion plus the freedom philosophy equals spiritual, intellectual, and material abundance. This book will focus on freedom and all of its components.

***"Man needs to be free in order that he may fulfill the demands of his nature, and his purpose in life."*** He must be free to serve his Creator properly. Freedom is a political implementation and conservation, or if need be, restoration and extension of the religious precepts of man. Faith and freedom are two sides of the same coin. Religious scholars should also be scholars in the philosophy of freedom.

There are two categories of freedom, the inner and the outer, the spiritual (remedies for personality defects) and the sociological (restraint of the misuse of government that causes man's inhumanity to man). They are connected with the spiritual being the primary goal and the sociological being the secondary goal.

The challenge for religious scholars is sifting through all the propaganda and lies about the five forms of government and three types of economic systems to analyze, compare and evaluate them for the greatest good for the greatest number of people. Religious scholars should realize that while they may be experts in one field, they could be totally ignorant in another—and *"that the more one learns, the more there is to learn."*

Too many religious scholars read their respective holy books *only*, and they think their search for knowledge is complete. However, it would be wise for them to realize that reading their respective scriptures is not the end but the beginning of knowledge, wisdom, and understanding. It provides the **key(s)** to the vicegerency of the entire universe. It unravels the mysteries of all that is needed for humankind to obtain optimal survival. Hopefully, they will be open-minded when studying the relationship between government and economics and freedom, which leads to optimal survival in this life and the hereafter.

People can't run from the truth. They can't hide from it. They just have to face it. They will have to put truth over politics and their love for people over their self-interest. Indeed, history will undoubtedly pull the cover off certain things that they might prefer to remain hidden. However, *"truth crushed to earth will someday rise again."*

This book is based on the premise that to restore freedom and then maintain it, champion and celebrate freedom, all of humankind must be thoroughly familiar with the various *forms* of government.

Human beings must also understand the proper function of economics in the development of government and its influences on the culture of its citizens. It is crucial that freedom-loving people know that the rights of life, liberty, and property originated with the Creator *before* governments ever existed and not *after* the establishment of governments. Frederic Bastiat explains this in his book *The Law* as follows:

> *"We hold from God the gift which includes all
> others. This gift is life — physical, intellectual,
> and moral life.*

> *"But life cannot maintain itself alone. The Creator
> of life has entrusted us with the responsibility of*

*preserving, developing, and perfecting it. In order that we may accomplish this, He has provided us with a collection of marvelous faculties. And He has put us in the midst of a variety of natural resources. By the application of our faculties to these natural resources we convert them into products, and use them. This process is necessary in order that life may run its appointed course.*

*"Life, faculties, production — in other words, individuality, liberty, property — this is man. And in spite of the cunning of artful political leaders, these three gifts from God precede all human legislation, and are superior to it. Life, liberty, and property do not exist because men have made laws. On the contrary, it was the fact that life, liberty, and property existed beforehand that caused men to make laws in the first place."*

Frederic Bastiat, "The Law"

The Relationship Between

# Government

# Economics

# And

# Freedom!

# PART ONE

## GOVERNMENTAL SYSTEMS

Law and Government is the collective organization of the individual's right to lawful defense.

*"Each of us has a natural right — from God — to defend his person, his liberty, and his property. These are the three basic requirements of life, and the preservation of any one of them is completely dependent upon the preservation of the other two. For what are our faculties but the extension of our individuality? And what is property but an extension of our faculties? If every person has the right to defend even by force — his person, his liberty, and his property, then it follows that a group of men have the right to organize and support a common force to protect these rights constantly. Thus the principle of collective right — its reason for existing, its lawfulness — is based on individual right. And the common force that protects this collective right cannot logically have any other purpose or any other mission than that for which it acts as a substitute. Thus, since an individual cannot lawfully use force against the person, liberty, or property of another individual, then the common force — for the same reason — cannot lawfully be used to destroy the person, liberty, or property of individuals or groups.*

*"Such a perversion of force would be, in both cases, contrary to our premise. Force has been given to us to defend our own individual rights. Who will dare to say that force has been given to us to destroy the equal rights of our brothers? Since no individual acting separately can lawfully use force to destroy the rights of others, does it not logically follow that the same principle also applies to the common force that is nothing more than the organized combination of the individual forces?*

*"If this is true, then nothing can be more evident than this: The law is the organization of the natural right of*

*lawful defense. It is the substitution of a common force for individual forces. And this common force is to do only what the individual forces have a natural and lawful right to do: to protect persons, liberties, and properties; to maintain the right of each, and to cause <u>justice</u> to reign over us all.*

*"If a nation were founded on this basis, order would prevail among the people, in thought as well as in deed. Such a nation would have the most simple, easy to accept, economical, limited, non-oppressive, just, and enduring government imaginable — whatever its political form might be.*

*"Under such an administration, everyone would understand that he possessed all the privileges as well as all the responsibilities of his existence. No one would have any argument with government, provided that his person was respected, his labor was free, and the fruits of his labor were protected against all unjust attacks. When successful, he would not have to thank the state for his success. And, conversely, when unsuccessful he would no more think of blaming the state for his misfortune than would the farmers blame the state because of hail or frost. The state would be felt only by the invaluable blessings of safety provided by this concept of government."*

Frederic Bastiat, "The Law"

# Chapter 1

## *The Five Basic Forms of Government*

*"Government is said to be a necessary evil. The saying appears to be without merit. For can anything be at once necessary and evil? True, all governments have had a history of evil-doing, more or less. However, it does not follow from this experience that their good is indistinguishable from their evil.*

*"Governments – assuming a proper limitation of their activities – are necessary and not evil. Their evil begins when they step out of bounds. The only necessity is that their evil actions be discontinued.*

*"Such an achievement is unlikely until the principles prescribing the boundary lines are searched for and found."*

Leonard E. Read, Founder of FEE

This book will explain the five forms of government. It is not about politics, which is the science of governing. Government is like a structure or a container. It is the foundation from which the contents of all politics and even cultures develop. For example, a glass is a container, and its water is the content. The glass is the structure that holds the content, shapes it, and prevents it from dispersing or spilling on the ground.

A *form* of government has a similar relationship to politics and the democratic process. The *form* of government is the container, and the politics and democratic processes are its contents. By democratic process, the author simply means the voting process (if voting is even allowed), by which elected officials are selected to 'run' the government *form* according to the supreme law of the land.

It is also based on the premise that individuals must be thoroughly familiar with the various forms of government to remain free and celebrate and champion freedom.

Members of society must also understand the proper function of economics in the development of government and its influences on the culture of its citizens. Freedom-loving people must know that the rights of life, liberty, and property originated with the Creator *before* governments ever existed, not *after* the establishment of governments.

This book will present and discuss the five basic forms of government. They are **Monarchy, Oligarchy, Democracy, Republic, and Anarchy.** The founding fathers established the republic form of government here in America. It will be examined and compared with the other four governmental *forms*.

All governmental forms from past antiquity to the present can fall within a spectrum of being limited in scope and power (or no government at all) on one end of the spectrum to totalitarian in power at the other. It matters not if one studies ancient Egypt, Mesopotamia, Ethiopia, Greece, or Rome. It does not matter whether one studies Asian history, European history, African history, or modern-day forms of government. Any and all of them from ancient times until today fall under one of the five *forms* of government, as explained in this book.

However, the name or label of government is not the most important indicator that determines if people are free. The size and amount of government on all levels (federal, state, and local) helps determine true freedom for each individual. Freedom for the collective is determined by how much freedom the individual has within the society or group. It takes individuals to make up a group. Therefore, if the individuals are free, then the group is free. And if there is no individual freedom, then the group is not free.

Two old related sayings should always be remembered. One is ***"Small people need big government, and big people need small government."*** The other is ***"governments govern best that governs the least."***

The true nature of government is based on a *'negation'* concept, meaning that the government does not promote anything. It simply removes the harmful elements from society. These negative elements include fraud, extortion, cheating, theft, murder, coercion, etc.

Good and law-abiding private citizens will create positive activity on their own, free of government interference. People's positive ideas and activities will be pursued based on their own personal interest in optimal survival, including the interest in their personal salvations in the hereafter. They could have, do, or be whatever they desire as long as it is peaceful.

When any government functions properly according to its true nature, peace and justice will reign. Citizens are free to do whatever is peaceful as long as they do not destroy (through fraud, extortion, force, or coercion) the life, liberty, or property of others. But freedom is not licentious, bestiality, or criminality! It should not lead to immoral or vulgar behavior.

With freedom, people are allowed to peacefully pursue their religious convictions based on the dictates of their own consciences. The government does not tax its citizens to support or promote any particular religious beliefs or institutions. Each respective religious community supports and promotes its own. As a result, none can charge the government with discrimination or favoring one religious community over another.

It should also be noted that the term 'government,' which is usually defined as 'to govern,' is a little misleading. The government's true nature and function are not to govern but to be a guardian, protector, or law enforcer. It is to remove bad characters, obstacles, and activities out of the way of free law-abiding citizens so they can live in peace and safety.

The government does NOT govern the individuals; individuals govern themselves through a proper understanding of ethics. ***Ethics***, according to L. Ron Hubbard ***"consists simply of the actions an individual takes on himself. It is a personal thing...."*** And justice only comes into play, according to him, ***"when the individual fails to put in his own ethics, the group takes action against him."*** This is done through some legal means, hopefully by due process.

When individuals ethically govern themselves, they make their own decisions, plan their own lives, and take responsibility for the consequences of their choices and plans. However, the term 'government' will be used throughout this work for the lack of a better word.

Good economics is essential to developing wealth and prosperity. It is the only way to eliminate poverty, starvation, homelessness, suffering, uncontrollable diseases, and unnatural deaths. It also helps to eliminate wars and solve the problem of racism.

It is essential that the right *form* of government is matched with its complementary type of economic system. If the match is not compatible, instead of progress, society will suffer deterioration, collapse, and be doomed to repeat this cycle.

The five basic forms of government and their corresponding economic systems will be explained in the simplest manner. Part One will cover the forms of government. Part Two will cover the types of economic systems.

*"He who would dare to undertake the political creation of a people ought to believe that he can, in a manner of speaking, transform human nature; transform each individual — who, by himself, is a solitary and perfect whole — into a mere part of a greater whole from which the individual will henceforth receive his life and being. Thus the person who would undertake the political creation of a people should believe in his ability to alter man's constitution; to strengthen it; to substitute for the physical and independent existence received from nature, an existence which is partial and moral. In short, the would-be creator of political man must remove man's own forces and endow him with others that are naturally alien to him."*

*"….it is not strange that…the human race was regarded as inert matter, ready to receive everything — form, face, energy, movement, life — from a great prince or a great legislator or a great genius … nourished on the study of antiquity. And antiquity presents everywhere — in Egypt, Persia, Greece, Rome — the spectacle of a few men molding mankind according to their whims, thanks to the prestige of force and of fraud. But this does not prove that this situation is desirable. It proves only that since men and society are capable of improvement, it is naturally to be expected that error, ignorance, despotism, slavery, and superstition should be greatest towards the origins of history." Today, the admirers of antiquity are "not in error when they found ancient institutions to be such, but they" are "in error when they offered them for the admiration and imitation of future generations. Uncritical and childish conformists, they" take "for granted the grandeur, dignity, morality, and happiness of the artificial societies of the ancient world. They do "not understand that knowledge appears and grows with the passage of time; and*

*that in proportion to this growth of knowledge, might takes
the side of right, and society regains possession of itself.*

*"...it is claimed that persons are nothing but raw material.
It is not for them to will their own improvement; they are
incapable of it...only the legislator is capable of doing this.
Persons are merely to be what the legislator wills them to
be....the legislator begins by decreeing the end for which the
commonwealth has come into being. Once this is determined,
the government has only to direct the physical and moral
forces of the nation toward that end. Meanwhile, the
inhabitants of the nation are to remain completely passive...
the people should have no prejudices, no affections, and
no desires except those authorized by the legislator."*

*Frederic Bastiat, "The Law"*

# Chapter 2

# *Monarchy*

*"Samuel told all the words of the LORD to the people who were asking him for a king. He said, "This is what the king who will reign over you will claim as his rights: He will take your sons and make them serve with his chariots and horses, and they will run in front of his chariots. Some he will assign to be commanders of thousands and commanders of fifties, and others to plow his ground and reap his harvest, and still others to make weapons of war and equipment for his chariots. He will take your daughters to be perfumers and cooks and bakers. He will take the best of your fields and vineyards and olive groves and give them to his attendants. He will take a tenth of your grain and of your vintage and give it to his officials and attendants. Your male and female servants and the best of your cattle and donkeys he will take for his own use. He will take a tenth of your flocks, and you yourselves will become his slaves. When that day comes, you will cry out for relief from the king you have chosen, but the LORD will not answer you in that day."*

*Bible Scripture: 1 Samuel 10-18*

The word Monarchy is derived from ancient Greek terminology. It is a combination of two words, "mono" and "arkhein." **Mono** means one or single, and **arkhein** means to rule. Together they mean one single ruler.

The essence of a monarchy is a dictatorship. It is the same as an autocratic or despotic government where a single ruler has absolute unrestricted power and authority. A despot is an individual who has *"absolute and arbitrary authority...independent of the control of other men."* Under a true monarchy, the political authority has an undivided rule. He has no associate and no partner to share his power.

He is looked upon as a god-king, a person preordained to lead. Eventually, limitations can be forced upon a monarchy until it is transformed into an oligarchy, another *form* of government (ruled by the few).

A monarchy is characterized as a **total**itarian or statist *form* of governmental rule. In such a government, one person rules by decree and executive orders. He has unlimited discretionary power, which is neither clearly defined nor limited. His power is absolute, and there are no laws that limit it. This power is generally either taken through conquest and force, perpetuated by an elitist group, or passed down by birthright. It can end in several ways; sometimes through conquest and force, sometimes through abdication, and at other times by the death of the monarch (either natural or by assassination).

When the 'rulership' is passed down by birth, it is called a hereditary monarchy. Those of a certain lineage or bloodline are believed to be of superior intellectual, spiritual, and sometimes physical strength. As a result, a royal family develops. Just as children inherit different forms of wealth from their parents, these royal families inherit wealth, power, AND people. Those that are inherited become known as the 'inherited people.'

The monarch is a ruler who is elevated to some type of imperial majesty status. This ruler is placed upon a pedestal and becomes the dominating personality in the lives of his subjects. It seems like the history and progress of his followers begin with him. His followers imagine that only he (the present ruler) is all-knowing and all-powerful. His words become law, and his 'wisdom' is considered supreme. His supporters become blind followers – an aggregation of human bodies without their own will. Human Automatons! All past heroes and leaders become a fading memory.

Next, they become 'volunteer' slaves and personality or celebrity worshipers, even though they will never admit it. Their daily discussions are about the ruler's personal attributes. They waste unnecessary energy discussing his lifestyle in frivolous details - what he likes, eats, wears, drives, where he vacations, and with whom, etc.

Under dictatorial rule, the governed have little or no input on who will govern them. The governed have very little or no individual freedoms. There is no 'Bill of Rights.' Under a monarchy, rights that should belong to the people are derived by and dependent on the leader. Independent thinking and individuality are discouraged and suppressed in favor of the monarch's views (or dictator) whom they are inclined to imitate. Henchmen surround him, and if anyone differs openly from the ruler, that person's life, livelihood, and perhaps that of his family could be in danger.

On the other hand, some dictators would try to give the appearance of democracy under their rule. They will occasionally handpick so-called party members, supporters, or an Ad Hoc committee, secure a hand count on a particular topic of discussion and call it a democratic vote. They promote this as true democracy. On a limited basis, for the leader's benefit, maybe it is a pinch of democracy.

This can work for a small organization or group but not for a more complex society or governmental system. It is a ruse to conceal the dictatorial powers' real tendencies. After all, he can still replace or dismiss those who disagree with him, or he may not invite them to future decision-making committees. He also has the privilege of forming these committees or disbanding them whenever, wherever, and however he pleases.

In close association with the monarchy, there are many individuals with characteristics becoming obsequious buffoons. They seem to have lost all sense of individuality, integrity, and common sense. These subject-minded individuals have traded all their dignity and self-respect for their loyalty to the ruler. They are dependents and liabilities, mesmerized and starstruck by him. These trusting souls are entirely overwhelmed by the mystique of the leader, which they consciously and unconsciously kowtow.

On any serious topic or discussion, these subject-minded followers will search every word of their ruler/savior before taking a position or having an opinion. Suppose their leader has ever (even decades before) mentioned the topic remotely or in any casual, frivolous manner. In that case, they take that as an absolute fact, indisputable truth, and the rule of law. For them, it is the end of the discussion. Now they feel relieved and justified. They become smug and arrogant. They no longer have to think for themselves.

This attraction goes beyond a person simply having more knowledge about a particular discipline than others; the subject-minded followers believe he is an expert on everything. It is indisputable that people who are experts in one subject area are equally ignorant in others, simply because no one knows all and no human being is perfect. It may sound good to say that almost anyone can be or do anything they want, but it is a fact that no one can be or do everything. Many people have more knowledge than others in a particular subject, but they are not praised by others every single day.

If the knowledge being taught is only on a theoretical or spiritual plane, then people's development will gradually decrease after a short while. This is because, after the initial surge of information from the leader, subsequent information will level off and slowly trickle down to an ineffective level. The leader will only rehash the same old information simply presented in a different way. And in many situations, he will redefine words with his own definitions and opinions. If nothing tangible or material results from the knowledge, then his followers will only become experts at longwinded rhetoric and oratory speech—all styles with little substance.

They will stagnate unless the followers are taught how to apply the knowledge and show tangible results. The real result will be a mass of mentally underdeveloped followers. The world will seldom acknowledge favorably a group of people who produce nothing concrete and will not respect people who have no commerce, institutions, organizations, or governance. They are people who only live to be led!

Even when the monarch speaks the truth, the blind followers will declare, *"Our leader always tells the truth and is always an honest person."* This may or may not have an ounce of real truth, but it is truth as the leader sees it. The problem is that there is an unlimited number of truths to be discovered in this universe and revealed by all mankind. And no one man can possibly have a monopoly on *all* truths.

There are new discoveries about the universe being made regularly. So, while the followers are fixated on the limited truths that come from this one leader, they miss out on the many other truths from other similarly smart and intelligent individuals. They also miss out on the tremendous amount of knowledge their own independent research and study can obtain.

Monarchs are dictatorial. They specialize in platitudes of beatitudes. Dictators have a reputation for making promises they cannot keep. They indulge heavily in nepotism and cronyism. Positions in government and other employment positions (under their influence) are filled based upon whom a person knows rather than what a person knows. There is no due process of law, only arbitrary and whimsical rule - usually based upon opinions, feelings, and emotions.

Under this scenario, the masses' intelligence is limited by one despotic individual's limited understanding and limited intelligence. It matters not whether he is tyrannical or benevolent. Even under the rule of a benevolent dictator, the people suffer economically and intellectually. They seldom advance to their fullest potential individually or as a group. All roads to personal distinction among the people are closed, except for a few acceptable to the ruler.

The dictatorial 'state apparatus' controls and regulates people, resources, capital, education, and the media. Every day decrees are made regarding what can or cannot be produced, consumed, taught, viewed, and heard. The dictator rules by deception, coercion, or force. He (alone) influences every aspect of the life of people; from what books and newspapers they can read, what movies or TV shows they can watch, and what music they can hear…he controls (by command or by suggestion) what news outlets they use.

He also influences what should be taught or not taught in schools and society in general. The dictator manages the economy and intervenes in it in the name of the 'state' *he* has established. Usually, total controls of the means of production, distribution, and consumption of all goods and services are in the hands of the *auto*cratic state. To control production, distribution, and consumption, the dictator has to control, by force, people and natural resources (land), labor, and capital. This is totalitarianism!

For centuries people believed that monarchs (pharaohs, kings, queens, etc.) were anointed with supernatural abilities – god-kings. They believed them to be true messengers from God with more wisdom than their subjects (followers) and even possessing magical powers. Some people even believed that the monarch could intercede for them with God. Others relied on the rulers to give them spiritual inspiration and emotional motivation and even heal them from certain diseases.

These people loved the ruler more than they loved God. They feared the king or queen more than they feared God, even though they claimed that they loved and feared God more. These subjects mastered the art of saying one thing while doing something else, which amounted to deceiving others and themselves at the same time.

Today, many people argue that a monarchy or dictatorship is the best *form* of governing. They claim that it is natural. They base this on the appearance of a traditional family structure where there is a father (dictator) and the wife and children (those dictated to).

However, in the real world, outside of the family structure, it is not the same as when grown men and women are created with equal opportunity by God (in terms of life, liberty, and the pursuit of happiness) and possess relatively similar potential. In a world where men are created equals by God, *or at least with equal opportunity,* no man has the right to dictate the personal lives of other men. No man has the right to proclaim that he has power and authority over others at all, especially for a lifetime.

Men are not the wives and children of other men, or one man. Men are not meant to be submissive or to allow someone else to think for them. They are not to forgo originality and creativity just to be imitators of someone else. Therefore, real men are not to be treated as wives and children of others. How can a man gain true love and respect from his wife and family when he is not his own man? In such a situation, he will be seen as another man's boy.

It is repugnant to see a man's character development retarded because he becomes too dependent on another as to how he should think, what he should say, and how he should act. To base dictatorship on the family, the structure is a weak and misleading argument. The points being made also apply to a female ruler.

Rather than being guided by high ideals, philosophies, and ideologies (or simply the will of the Creator), a cult following revolves around a personality. Even if one wants to get to heaven or seek the truth about the Creator, it is suggested by fellow followers that the only way to get there is through the particular ruler. The monarch's words and interpretations become de facto law.

The ruler is discussed intensively and extensively while alive and usually debated about years after he dies or until another ruler takes his place. Because the 'personality leadership' becomes so huge in the eyes of his followers, their entire struggle or mission becomes embodied in one individual. The followers lose sight of the real struggle around them and forget that the struggle for advancement is bigger than any one person.

Instead of the Creator, the personality leader becomes the center of attraction and attention. Meanwhile, no workable program, plan, or solution is presented for the masses to implement for their progress and success. The leader may talk about the desired effects or his personal goals, but he is evasive about an effective process to achieve them. There are never clear, definite, and achievable strategies or plans established for people to hold on to after the leader dies.

When the leader dies, the followers have to start all over again with another personality leader. They will be on the lookout for one without a doubt because they are insecure and weak when it comes to being independent thinkers and self-motivated individuals. They are looking for their 'conquer me' moment, and they search for a 'strong hand' with words to tickle their ears.

These personality leaders are well taken care of in terms of fortune and fame, but the masses who follow them continue to suffer. The leader does everything to empower himself—but very little, if anything, to empower the masses. The most they get from a personality leader is vague and weak recommendations that are already commonly known in the first place, just mere opinions.

A strong community is a reflection of strong and wise leadership. And a weak community is a reflection of weak and unwise leadership or of someone who simply does not care for those who follow him. He neither cares about their present condition nor their future.

As to those who claim to be God-fearing, the author believes it is hypocritical. It is an insult to the All-Powerful and All-Knowing Creator for them to give this kind of power and authority over themselves to any other mortal human being. Power and authority of this kind belong solely to God.

Many of these same people argue that dictatorship is what the prophets of God brought to humankind, as if it has some divine relevance. God has said He would not dictate to man. He has given man free will to make individual choices. So why does a dictator feel that it is his (divine) right to dictate to another human being?

Dictatorships are ancient. They are not new inventions. When the prophets of God were born, all of them were born under some pre-existing dictatorship. According to history and scriptures, dictatorships preceded all of the prophets of God. And these dictatorships were evil, wicked, and oppressive by nature. They were so corrupt that people generally suffered in ignorance, superstition, poverty, and disease. They suffered mentally, emotionally, materially, physically, and spiritually.

God sent the prophets to destroy these dictatorial powers, set the people free, and teach them to fear God and accept His authority and guidance only. He guided them mainly through the Word of God. The prophets did not instruct the people to set up any particular form of government. They did not leave any clear, distinct, or permanent form of government for a whole nation, especially not for the entire world to follow—a world that includes different races, cultures, and climates. The people would have to figure out for themselves the best *form* of government under which to live, one that would be just and secure for their freedom of conscience, peace of mind, and prosperity and growth.

As long as a government protects life, liberty, property, and the pursuit of happiness and allows for freedom of religious worship, this should be enough. Otherwise, if the government were to get more involved than this, it would risk establishing a 'state' religion.[1] A state religion or theocracy would be the result of no separation at all between state and religion. A theocracy means 'The state's monopoly of religion.' It is when the state dictates, controls, and finances a particular religion by taxing, one way or another, all citizens to

---

1    State as in a country or sovereign political government. Thus, it refers to the official religion as deemed by the government.

support the state religion, regardless of each individual's convictions or beliefs.

Even if it is not their own, people of different faiths would be taxed to maintain or perpetuate the state religion. The state religion would grow stronger and stronger until it suppresses the non-state religions and even prohibits or oppress the weaker faiths. This would not be fair or just to those who do not adhere to the state's monopoly on religion. This would amount to coercion in religion. And in religion, there should be no coercion.

A theocracy would not work in America or any other pluralistic society. In a pluralistic society such as America, there has to be a separation of state and religion. Otherwise, there would be a conflict of interest between the different religious groups. It undoubtedly would lead to strife, anger, and bloodshed. This is because the state monopoly of religion would perennially tax the general public (including all the different faiths) to perpetuate itself.

Each religious community will sponsor and support its chosen politician(s) and commission them to go to the public trough and get their share from it. Others will feel discriminated against and resent the national state religion. Religion will become even more political and more and more oppressive. Instead of it being a lodestar for freedom, it will become a force for oppression and slavery.

History has shown that state monopoly religion will use the state's police powers to suppress, oppress, persecute, and enslave others of different faiths. The only way that people can freely practice their respective religious faiths is that the government is not involved, except to protect them from any threats or actual harm to their lives, liberties, and properties.

As with individuals, the various religious faiths should support limited government and personal responsibility. When individuals (and their respective religious communities) exercise personal responsibility, there will be no resources taken by the state from one religious group and given to another.

Even in state facilities or on state premises, religious groups could be allowed to display their symbols within their local communities when paid for with their own private and local monies while following established rules and guidelines.

In most cases, the prophets of God did not even appoint a particular successor. Could they have meant for people to solve this problem of limited leadership for themselves? Could it have been that they thought it was perfectly acceptable for humanity to establish *any form* of government it deemed just and workable, as long as God and His laws were not contradicted?

As a result, the people (the governed) could review, research, and establish the best *form* of government conducive to their freedom, peace, prosperity, advancement, and dignity. This gives people integrity, *"the accurate reflection in word and deed of whatever one's highest conscience dictates as righteous."*

The government could be administrated by men but not ruled by men. The government would be based on God's laws AND the laws of nature. These laws would be compatible with freedom, justice, and equal opportunity for all. And the government would be ruled by law.

A monarchic *form* of government is compatible with fascist, Nazi, socialist, and communist economic systems. Many kinds of monarchies exist, including kingdoms, theocracies, chiefdoms, tribes, etc. Rulers of these monarchies are called pharaohs, kings, queens, emperors, Caesars, czars, emirs, chiefs, etc.

> *"It is not true that the masses are always right and know the means for attaining the ends aimed at. "Belief in the common man" is no better founded than was belief in the supernatural gifts of kings, priests, and noblemen.... Majorities too may err and destroy our civilization. The good*

*cause will not triumph merely on account of its reasonableness and expediency. Only if men are such that they will finally espouse policies reasonable and likely to attain the ultimate ends aimed at, will civilization improve and society and state render men more satisfied, although not happy in a metaphysical sense."*

Ludwig Von Mises, "Human Action"

## *A Prayer From My Heart*

Dear Lord,
Deliver me from dictators
And egotistical narcissistic men
Who wants to control my mind
And force me into sin.
They try to create hatred, anger, and strife,
Condemn my every thought,
Dictate what I should believe
And regiment my life.
They suck up all my time
While I'm still in my prime,
So they can use me
To do their bidding,
But never give me a dime.
They claim to be my friend,
To think and make decisions for me,
So in their *leaderless* leadership
I will always depend.
They say I need them
To lead me around
Like a puppet on a string,
While they look at me
With arrogance
And anoint themselves, my king!

*By Kariem A. Haqq*

# Charismatic Leadership



*"Ah, you miserable creatures! You who think that you are so great! You who judge humanity to be so small! You who wish to reform everything! Why don't you reform yourselves? That task would be sufficient enough."*

*Frederic Bastiat, "The Law"*

A monarchic *form* of government is not to be confused with the charismatic leadership of an organization or a group of people. A monarch is over a nation. Charismatic leadership is not necessarily a ruler over any government. This leadership type is usually not allowed in a monarchic or despotic *form* of government. Under a monarchy, there is no tolerance for competitive, comparatively 'strong' leadership that could pose a conflict or potential threat to the dictator in power.

All organizations and their charismatic leaders (if allowed to exist at all) are, to some extent, under the control and regulation of the dictator. Organizational charismatic leadership usually exists in a free society, not a totalitarian one. Charismatic leadership over organizations or various movements often supports the government. However, some grow to be antagonistic towards it and strive to change or replace it. They are characterized as revolutionaries, rebels, militants, and protestors.

There is an old belief that weak people who cannot think rationally or act responsibly need a strong dictatorial government or charismatic leader to exert his authority over them. Those with this belief think only in terms of sheep-dogs and shepherds who must herd the feckless sheep.

These sheeple prefer to be selfless nonentities who adhere to the philosophy of Plato. It is attributed to him to have stated:

*"The greatest principle of all is that nobody,
whether male or female, should be without
a leader. Nor should the mind of anybody be
habituated to letting him do anything at all on
his own initiative; neither out of zeal, nor even
playfully. But in war and in the midst of peace—
to his leader he shall direct his eye and follow
him faithfully. And even in the smallest matter
he should stand under leadership. For example,
he should get up, or move, or wash, or take his
meals ... only if he has been told to do so. In a
word, he should teach his soul, by long habit,
never to dream of acting independently, and to
become utterly incapable of it."*

On the other hand, strong people who are independent thinkers, self-motivated, and act responsibly need weak, limited government, or they need 'organizational' type leaders more than 'charismatic' ones. Their mentalities are more on the line advocated by Leonard E. Read, Founder of FEE:

*"I wish to be free from dictators – all of
them – be they of the one-man variety or an
agglomeration hiding behind an act of Congress
or an administrative ruling that restrains creative
actions. Leave me free to do anything I please –
stupid or brilliant – so long as it is peaceful and
not injurious to others. Let me work at whatever
I please for whatever I can obtain by willing
exchange, whether the wage be a mere trifle or
a king's ransom. Let my hours of labor range
as I please from zero to 168 per week – subject,
of course, to contracts....Free me from those
people who would attend to my welfare, not with
the fruits of their own labor in the voluntary*

> *practice of charity, but with the collective exacted*
> *income of others. (People who legalize theft via*
> *taxation beyond benefits received by those taxed,*
> *then sanctify it and call it charity.) My welfare*
> *is no one else's business; it is a matter between*
> *me and my God, not between those who levy and*
> *those who pay taxes. Finally, free me from fraud,*
> *violence, misrepresentation, and thievery – the*
> *destructive actions of men – the curbing of which*
> *is the sole role I would assign to government."*

*Leonard E. Read, "Having My Way"*

Strong, independent, and self-reliant-minded people cannot function in an environment where someone constantly tries to dictate, control, or limit their creative thinking. They feel God gave them the right to think independently and make choices in their best interest, as long as they do not destroy someone else's life, liberty, or property. Any other situation established by control, intimidation, and coercion would lead to some forms of oppression and slavery.

The best leadership having the best intentions can only give the highlights in terms of knowledge and understanding. It is up to the individual followers to fill in the details. But most individuals take the highlights as the details and the superficial as the actual or real. After giving many details regarding faith and ethics, even the greatest religious books only guide us to the full knowledge of life, death, and the universe. God speaks to humanity about the fish in the oceans and seas, but it is up to humankind to discover and name the many different life forms they discover in them and estimate their value.

God speaks about the animals He created, but it is up to man to learn about their features, habits, and worth. God speaks about the birds, mountains, rivers, lakes, etc., but man must learn about their locations and natures. God speaks of eating good food and living in good homes, but people must learn for themselves the details of how to fish, hunt, grow food, cook food, and build good homes. The Almighty speaks of science, law, history, trade, industry, etc., but it is up to humanity to find out the details of these subjects and apply them for the benefit of all.

Some individual followers stumble over the highlights and take them as supreme knowledge. They fail to realize that there is so much more to learn. God guides through His word, and the best leaders only give highlights. It is up to individuals to do independent research and study for the details. If they fail in this responsibility, they will not mature as men and women, and they will neither grow intellectually nor make material progress.

Most followers are entirely mesmerized by charismatic leadership and become totally dependent on it. They only follow the path of self-deception, idleness, and mental lethargy, believing that they have the details when they only have the highlights. There is revealed knowledge by God. And there is unrevealed knowledge that has to be discovered by man. People should spend less time studying individual leaders and more time studying God's natural laws and His many systems of knowledge.

In his excellent book, Human Action, Ludwig Von Mises talked about the followers of these consecrated leaders. He said: ***"They pretend that their leaders are blessed by a knowledge inaccessible to the rest of mankind and contrary to the ideas maintained by those to whom the charisma is denied. The charismatic leaders have been entrusted by a mystical higher power with the office of managing the affairs of erring mankind. They alone are enlightened; all other people are either blind and deaf or malefactors."***

> ***"Hero-worship is strongest where there is least regard for human freedom."***
>
> *Herbert Spencer*

# Chapter 3

# *Oligarchy*

*"From the day when the first members of councils placed exterior authority higher than interior, that is to say, recognized the decisions of men united in councils (committees) as more sacred than reason and conscience; on that day began the lies that caused the loss of millions of human beings and which continue their unhappy work to the present day."*

*Leo Tolstoy*

Oligarchy comes from two words, "oligos' and "arkheim." "Oligos" simply means "a few." "Arkheim" means "to rule" or "to command." Combined, we get the word Oligarchy. Plutocracy is a type of oligarchy in which the rich few rule the masses of the people.

The oligarchic *form* of government is similar to a monarchy. It is also dictatorial, totalitarian, and statist. Statism is a general belief that the 'State' (centralized control) should control and regulate either economic or social policy.

Under oligarchy, instead of one person being the ruler like in a monarchy, a small selected few rules through the government apparatus with full police powers. These few officials represent aristocratic, elitist, intellectual, military, or religious clans. They are a relatively small handful of individuals who use the government to control and regulate the majority of the people, their resources, and the media. They have the power to control the wealth of the land,

and they always look out for themselves, their families, and their friends first.

Oligarchies throughout history have been known to be one of the more stable *forms* of government, but not necessarily the most prosperous. They are still known for very little individual freedom. Under this *form* of government, 'a few' use the state to *manage* the economy through interventions, regulations, and controls. Total control of the means of production, distribution, and consumption is in the hands of the state's governing body. The governed have little or no input into who will govern them or how they will be governed.

An oligarchic *form* of government is compatible with fascist, Nazis, socialist, and communist economic systems. Again, like all totalitarian governments, charismatic leadership of organizations or movements is not tolerated and is severely suppressed.

# Chapter 4

# *Democracy*

*"Democracy is the most vile form of government...
democracies have ever been spectacles of
turbulence and contention: have ever been found
incompatible with personal security or the rights
of property: and have in general been as short
in their lives as they have been violent in their
deaths."*

James Madison
(Father of the U.S. Constitution)

*In democracy ... there are commonly tumults
and disorders. ... Therefore a pure democracy is
generally a very bad government. It is often the
most tyrannical government on earth.*

Noah Webster

The majority of people rule in a democratic *form* of government. The word democracy has its roots in the Greek language. It combines two Greek words: "demo" meaning people, and "cracy" meaning rule. Combined, they mean the "people rule" or the "majority of the people rule." In a pure democracy, no representatives represent the masses. The masses or majority represent themselves on every issue and in every issue. The majority comprises at least 51 percent or more people, and the minority is 49 percent or less.

This narrow loss can lead to a large unhappy minority. When the margin of victory is very close, the potential for suspicion and conflict is significantly increased. This can be hard to overcome or accept by the losers. The two equally opposing forces clash and struggle until there is violence and chaos. Because of it, democracies almost always become unstable forms of government. Democracy is a form of government that leads to 'mobocracy' and 'anarchy,' accompanied by internal strife and violence.

> *The experience of all former ages had shown that of all human governments, democracy was the most unstable, fluctuating and short-lived.*
>
> *John Quincy Adams*

A major problem in society today is that people do not distinguish between the concept of democracy as a *form* of government and the concept of the **'democratic process'** as used for voting purposes within a pre-established constitutional republic *form* of government. In the latter case, the republic provides the structure. The 'democratic process' provides the method of electing or selecting the personnel to 'run' the basic structure as outlined in the republic's constitution.

The ***'democratic process'*** leads to the ballot box.

Structure and processes are similar to a container and its content. A glass can represent the container as compared to a government *form* or structure. The water in the glass can represent the content as compared to **'democratic processes.'** The container will give stability, shape, and form. The processes represent the flow and operational procedures. However, without the container (structure), the contents will spill over and be wasted. It is imperative that the form/structure/container is established first before the content (processes) is poured into it. The container has to exist before the content can exist.

A democracy is a *form* of government where people rule. It may or may not have a constitution, and it simply is where the majority rules on every decision, and the minority may not have any voice, rights, or protection.

**"Democracy is necessarily despotism"**

*Immanuel Kant*

On the other hand, the democratic process (actual voting) is simply a method of selecting individuals to run a particular type of government. The democratic processes should have pre-established laws (constitution). It should be exercised according to established laws such as the Constitution of the United States of America.

The democratic process is rational and practical for appropriate positions and issues. It is made effective through the ballot box. But pure democracy leads to mobocracy and results in people taking to 'the streets' to force their way, and their protest turns chaotic, uncontrollable, and violent.

**"Democracy... while it lasts is more bloody than either aristocracy or monarchy. Remember, democracy never lasts long. It soon wastes, exhausts, and murders itself. There is never a democracy that did not commit suicide."**

*John Adams*

# Chapter 5

# *Constitutional Republic*

***Outside Independence Hall when the
Constitutional Convention of 1787 ended, Mrs.
Powel of Philadelphia asked Benjamin Franklin:
"Well, Doctor, what have we got, a republic or
a monarchy?" With no hesitation whatsoever,
Franklin responded: "A republic, if you can
keep it."***

In the Constitutional Republic, the society is ruled by a 'thing,' not by the people. That 'thing' is called 'law.' Once a society adopts a constitution under a republican *form* of government, it gives that constitution authority and power to rule, even when the real power ultimately resides in the people since they have the ultimate ability to amend it or abolish it. Any changes made should be in accordance with the process established by the constitution itself. Otherwise, 'law' no longer rules—the people do.

Society is ruled by law, with no one individual or group being above the law, even if that group is the majority of its citizens. Everyone is equal under the law, including the ruler(s), and no one is above the law, including the ruler(s). Under a constitutional republic, there are usually three branches of government: the executive, the legislative, and the judicial. They form a system of 'checks and balances.' Each of these three government functions is designed to check and balance the power of the other two branches. Each has the limited authority to approve, disapprove, or influence one another's power and influence within the constitutional boundaries.

The word 'Republic' comes from the Latin language. It is a combination of two Latin words; "res," which means a thing, and "public," which means "belonging to the public." Combined, they are "res_public" (republic), or "thing public," or "the public thing." 'Thing,' in this case, represents the law or the constitution. It is not a living person or group of people.

The constitution is the supreme law of the land or *the mother of all civil and legislative laws*. The constitution is simply the rule of law evolved into a codified and advanced form of law. All people (including individuals and the majority) must conform to this constitution (law). All other laws legislated or adjudicated must conform to this basic law of the land. If they conflict with the supreme law, they must be ruled unconstitutional or illegal. Again, no one (regardless of race, gender, age, religion, etc.) should be above the law. Not the ordinary citizen, nor the highest official(s) – presidents included.

The rule of law should be limited in scope. This ensures that people can maximize their own freedoms. Again, the government should be limited and also decentralized. Otherwise, people lose their freedoms in direct proportion to the increase in the scope of law and government.

The decentralized components (states) should be strong and subject to competition among themselves. The centralized component (national) should be weaker and have only enumerated authority. Neither should unjustly destroy the life, liberty, or property of anyone!

When there is limited government, there are few intrusions in the everyday decisions of each citizen, and there is a minimum amount of intervention in the private economy.

Individuals will be allowed to pursue happiness in whatever manner they choose as long as it is peaceful and not destroying the lives, liberties, or properties of others. Individual citizens or families will be responsible for their own successes or failures, and they will no longer blame the government or politicians for their successes or failures. This is because neither the government nor politicians will be involved in the everyday decision-making of individuals or their families.

Representative government is when people in different regions send a small contingent of individual(s) to local, state, or national capitals to represent them. These individuals are selected (or elected) via the democratic process called voting. They are representatives and represent the people who selected them through the election process.

According to the constitution itself, the democratic process is the method used to elect or hire the personnel needed to run the constitutional republic. This way, the person elected or hired to run the government is by the consent of the governed. Once these individuals are chosen, they are free to make decisions on behalf of the people who chose them.

These individual representatives make decisions and laws that govern the people. The majority (of the people) do not make these laws. The majority voted for these individuals by way of the democratic process to represent them. But the majority's decision-making activity stops after the voting process ends. Now, the representatives, also called legislators, will directly make decisions and laws on behalf of the majority. These decisions are always made first in accordance with the basic law of the land, not even based upon the will of the people nor by any polls. The laws should reflect the will of the people, but not if they go against the supreme law of the land (the Constitution).

Suppose these representatives make decisions or laws the majority does not approve of or deem unconstitutional. In that case, the only power the majority now has is voting them out of office. In addition, the Executive Branch can veto specific laws, and the Judicial Branch can rule them unconstitutional. Besides, the recall or impeachment process can be exercised according to the supreme law to remove individual representatives from office if necessary.

However, the democratic process does not mean very much if, by law, the citizens have only one candidate or one party's candidates for whom to vote. The choices of whom to vote for would be limited. Under a totalitarian regime, if some voters do not vote for a particular candidate or party's candidates, they are punished.

Also, the voting process is weak when the education received by the people is overwhelmingly public. Under these conditions, education and all academic decision-making are relatively centralized and dictated by a federal government. When the majority of the public (citizens) receive their education from centralized academia controlled by the government, public education compromises voter independence and weakens the voting process. Ignorant people vote for ignorant rulers!

In this case, the masses are taught only what the state wants them to know from pre-school through college. Most of the time, they are dummied down to vote against their own interest for the wrong people, issues, and reasons. This is how tyrants, socialists, and evil people come into power under a so-called democratic *form* of government. People will vote for politicians who make them promises of more (free) gifts and goodies from the government. They will vote for a bigger and bigger government and eventually vote themselves into slavery. *"Ignorant and free can never be!"*

A republic *form* is not a democracy *form*, nor is it the *'democratic processes.'* The last term is not interchangeable with the former. The *form* represents structure, shape, and organization. Electing personal to manage it is done through the fluid voting process and sometimes by appointments. The *form* is similar to a container, and the 'democratic process' is similar to the content. The container is not the same as the content.

If the container is a glass and the content is water, the glass is not the water, nor the water the glass. The republic *form* of government is not the same as *the 'democratic process'* (the method used to elect the personal/politicians). After being elected, politicians do appoint bureaucrats to help run the Republic *form* of government.

America's *form* of government is a republic. It is a form of government, but it is neither a republican democracy nor a democratic republic. America is a constitutional republic *form* of government that is based on rule by law. That 'law' is the constitution—the supreme law of the land.

In a government that is ruled by law, the only people who vote are those who pay the taxes that support the government. Also, the taxes are only collected from real property, not income. And collected on natural resources, but not improvements.

Under a republic, only taxpayers vote on issues involving 'money.' Therefore, only property owners are allowed to vote, especially on tax issues. This is to ensure that those who do not own property nor pay taxes are also not allowed to vote on issues that will tax money out of the pockets of those who do pay, with the intent of transferring tax money into the pockets of those (usually themselves) who do not pay taxes.

A republic usually remains stable until it degenerates into a democracy, eventually leading to anarchy.

Economic (private) agencies should be established to advise all three branches of government. They should be solely responsible for exposing and negating artificial laws that conflict with free market or free trade economic, natural laws. Their purpose should be to promote a minimum amount of government intervention and regulation of the economy. Working in conjunction with legislatures, they should check and expose labor unions, associations, and any business practices that are anti-free market. All anti-free market practices are discriminatory.

These private agencies should promote fewer government businesses and more private enterprises. They should encourage sound 'money' (a 'wealth medium of exchange), free trade, lower taxes, and be on the watch for government encroachment into the economic sphere. They should not be controlled by or be under any of the three branches, but they should support the Constitution and the checks and balances of all governmental power.

Another important agency is the private Free Press. It is called out or implied in the constitution. The free press is the watchdog for the citizens. It exposes lies and corruption in government.

America was meant to be a Republic - a "Constitutional Republic!" It's in the Pledge of Allegiance:

***"I pledge allegiance to the flag of the United States of America, and to the Republic for which it stands: one Nation under God, indivisible, with liberty and justice for all."***

**Chapter 6**

---

# *Anarchy*

**Anarchy is born when citizens 'take the law into their own hands.' The end of this road is the big, strong man."**

Leonard E. Read, Founder of FEE

Anarchy (unplanned chaos) exists in a society where individuals struggle only for themselves, their families, or their clan, resulting in an autonomous rule. Autonomous rule is when there is no government and individuals are forced into anarchy. In such a situation, individuals and small groups are self-governing. Each individual is the protector of himself, his family, or associates.

There is no official government for society as a whole. People must do it themselves if they need protections for their lives, liberties, and properties. They may act as individuals or organize into gangs, mobs, militias, etc. They engage in evil and criminal activity when they take other people's lives, liberties, or properties by force, fraud, or coercion. Even if they (the do-gooders) give/transfer by force the property of one party over to another party whom they 'feel' needs it more, it is still criminal.

The beginning of anarchy can be traced back to simple protest movements that turned into violent revolutionary movements intending to overthrow an established government. Simple and peaceful protests are reasonable and legal in a free society. But when a few try to bypass the due process of law and disrupt or shut down the whole community, they cross the boundary of justice and violate the rights of others to life, liberty, and property. Now protests become unjust, not just.

But people often get confused between protest and demand.

Generally speaking, a protest is *a statement or action expressing disapproval of something or an objection to something. It is to express an objection to what someone has said or done.* When done peacefully and without violating anyone else's rights, protest serves a positive purpose.

Demand, on the other hand, is different. Demand is *an insistent and peremptory request, made as if by right;* it is to *request or to ask for something.* It goes further than protest when *insisting on immediate attention or obedience.*

Both protest and demand are trying to get the government to act. The former tries to get the government to do its job and refrain from overstepping its constitutional authority by removing harmful elements or situations from the social environment. The latter is trying to get the government to do something not within its constitutional authority to do, mainly for expediency and appearance's sake, without due process of law.

There is a difference between protesting injustice and demanding justice. Neither can be done until after due process. But when protest crosses the line by stopping protests and start demanding, freedom and democracy turn into mobocracy and anarchy, resulting in a complete breakdown in society, chaos, and oppression.

This happens when inactive people suddenly become emotionally reactive. They seldom are intellectually proactive. They seldom analyze the root of the problem correctly or take any responsibility for correcting their contributions to the problem.

Naïve protesters who join protest movements become professional protesters. They make the protest a profession and anarchy a career. Their lives consist of only looking for things to protest. They live off victims (dead or alive) like a vampire lives off blood. And if they don't have a victim to exploit (or use), they will create one. This is their mindset, and this is their attitude. And the majority of literature they read is only to feed and reinforce disruption and destruction.

These anarchists are never involved in proactive planning to build positive and strong institutions or governments. This is because they are too busy trying to tear down everything with which they disagree.

Anarchy usually leads to monarchy as people call for a 'strong hand' to bring about law and order. Then monarchy slowly transforms into an oligarchy, which gradually leads to democracy, and quickly and violently leads back to anarchy.

Under anarchy, the people suffer because of confusion, chaos, and lack of government law and order. Then the cycle repeats—monarchy—>oligarchy—>democracy—>anarchy! How long in each process and how much destruction and suffering are incurred by the people varies.

In the meantime, the people experience poverty, war, and a lack of freedom and prosperity. This can occur in direct relation to the increase in size and amount of government, or no government at all. There has to be the right amount of government, usually small in scope, guaranteeing freedom for the people. Freedom requires "limited government," not anarchy (or no government at all), and certainly not totalitarianism.

In summary, four *forms* of government involve 'people rule,' whether as an individual, a few, a majority, or a mob. These four *forms* are monarchy, oligarchy, democracy, and anarchy. By definition, only the one republic form of government involves a 'thing' (law/constitution) that rules. It rules over the individual, the few, the majority, and against the mob.

***"Limit the Government, Not the People"***

*There is no perfect world. There has never been nor ever will be. There is no perfect "free market" economic system, and there is no perfect socialist/ communist economic system. What is true is that civilization will advance further the more society embraces the "free market," limited government, and personal responsibility, and civilization will decline faster the more society embraces Socialism/Communism.*

Kariem Abdul Haqq

# PART TWO

## ECONOMIC SYSTEMS

*"...law by no means confines itself to its proper functions. And when it has exceeded its proper functions, it has not done so merely in some inconsequential and debatable matters. The law has gone further than this; it has acted in direct opposition to its own purpose. The law has been used to destroy its own objective: It has been applied to annihilating the justice that it was supposed to maintain; to limiting and destroying rights which its real purpose was to respect. The law has placed the collective force at the disposal of the unscrupulous who wish, without risk, to exploit the person, liberty, and property of others. It has converted plunder into a right, in order to protect plunder. And it has converted lawful defense into a crime, in order to punish lawful defense... The law has been perverted by the influence of two entirely different causes: stupid greed and false philanthropy."*

*"Self-preservation and self-development are common aspirations among all people. And if everyone enjoyed the unrestricted use of his faculties and the free disposition of the fruits of his labor, social progress would be ceaseless, uninterrupted, and unfailing.*

*"But there is also another tendency that is common among people. When they can, they wish to live and prosper at the expense of others. This is no rash accusation. Nor does it come from a gloomy and uncharitable spirit. The annals of history bear witness to the truth of it: the incessant wars, mass migrations, religious persecutions, universal slavery, dishonesty in commerce, and monopolies. This fatal desire has its origin in the very nature of man — in that primitive, universal, and insuppressible instinct that impels him to satisfy his desires with the least possible pain."*

*"Man can live and satisfy his wants only by ceaseless labor; by the ceaseless application of his faculties to natural resources. This process is the origin of property.*

*"But it is also true that a man may live and satisfy his wants by seizing and consuming the products of the labor of others. This process is the origin of plunder.*

*"Now since man is naturally inclined to avoid pain — and since labor is pain in itself — it follows that men will resort to plunder whenever plunder is easier than work. History shows this quite clearly. And under these conditions, neither religion nor morality can stop it.*

*"When, then, does plunder stop? It stops when it becomes more painful and more dangerous than labor.*

*"It is evident, then, that the proper purpose of law is to use the power of its collective force to stop this fatal tendency to plunder instead of to work. All the measures of the law should protect property and punish plunder."*

Fredric Bastiat, "The Law

---

# Chapter 7

# *Three Types of Economics Systems*

*"A science of economics must be developed
before a science of politics can be logically
formulated. Essentially, economics is the science
of determining whether the interests of human
beings are harmonious or antagonistic. This
must be known before a science of politics can be
formulated to determine the proper functions of
government.*

*"Immediately following the development of a
science of economics, and at the very beginning
of the formulation of a science of politics, this
all-important question must be answered: What
is law? What ought it to be? What is its scope; its
limits? Logically, at what point do the just powers
of the legislator stop?*

*"I do not hesitate to answer:* **Law is the common
force organized to act as an obstacle of injustice.
*In short,* law is justice."**

Frederic Bastiat, "The Law"

Economics is the science of efficiently getting the most out of limited resources at any given time to satisfy unlimited wants and desires during that same limited time frame. Over the long term, resources are relatively limited. However, wants and desires are always unlimited in the short and long run.

Again, economic theory deals with how to solve the problem of satisfying unlimited wants and desires with scarce or limited resources within a given time frame. And within a reasonable time frame. It is a problem that has permeated the actions of humankind through the ages. It takes up the majority of man's thoughts, energy, and time.

Free-market economics always fosters tendencies that ensure things are being done in an efficient and timely manner. It results in lower prices, higher quality, and many choices of goods and services.

This theory of limited resources vs. unlimited wants can be applied individually or on a household basis. It can be applied in domestic or international businesses. The theory of economics can also be applied to the local, state, and national government levels. This is why people study personal finance, household or home economics, national and international business economics, public finance (economics), etc. They all want to learn how to economize or get the most out of their limited resources. And they all want to do it in an efficient and timely manner.

Solving the economic problems of scarcity on the national level is the focus of this chapter. However, individual, household, business, and state economics are tied to the national. Yet, the national is the result of or made-up of the individual, household, and business economies. They are different only in the sense that they are dependent on the national economic system of any given country.

The individual, household, and business economies differ in the sense that the national economic system is like the soil (mother earth). And the others are what grows out of it. If the soil is not fertile and cultivated properly but instead is corrupt, then nothing will grow healthy or wealthy.

Some people understand business very well, but they do not understand national and international economics. These particular individuals sometimes think that their harvest is all about them - their intelligence and skills. They believe that their successes are due to their own personal efforts only. They fail to realize that most of their success depends on the good soil (economic principles) within which they have to work. *It is the type of economic system, not the form of government that promotes economic wellbeing.* If the economic system is corrupt, then individual businesses in the community will not prosper.

Prosperity or the elimination of poverty is a by-product of freedom. A by-product does not have its origin in itself. It has its origin in something superior to it. Therefore, freedom (limited government, free-market economics, personal responsibility, and God Consciousness) is the origin and should be the primary goal and focus if humans want to eliminate poverty.

The three types of Economic Systems are:

- Free Market

- Socialism and its many shades (Feudalism, Mercantilism, Fascism, Nazism, and Socialism Proper)

- Communism

*There are doctrines flatly denying that there can be a science of economics. What is taught nowadays at most of the universities under the label of economics is practically a denial of it."*

**Ludwig Von Mises, "Human Action"**

# *My Creed*

*I do not choose to be a common man,*
*It is my right to be uncommon ... if I can,*
*I seek opportunity ... not security.*
*I do not wish to be a kept citizen.*
*Humbled and dulled by having the*
*State look after me.*
*I want to take the calculated risk;*
*To dream and to build.*
*To fail and to succeed.*
*I refuse to barter incentive for a dole;*
*I prefer the challenges of life*
*To the guaranteed existence;*
*The thrill of fulfillment*
*To the stale calm of Utopia.*
*I will not trade freedom for beneficence*
*Nor my dignity for a handout*
*I will never cower before any master*
*Nor bend to any threat.*
*It is my heritage to stand erect.*
*Proud and unafraid;*
*To think and act for myself,*
*To enjoy the benefit of my creations*
*And to face the world boldly and say:*
*This, with God's help, I have done*
*All this is what it means*
*To be an Entrepreneur.*

Dean Alfange

# Chapter 8

# *Free Market Economy*

*"Free Market: one in which the public is able to exchange production or service by competitive bidding, open to all, in the absence of government restriction against any commodity that is not directly restricted by the people themselves in open referendum."*

*Merrill Jenkins Sr.*

*"Free Enterprise: The ability to direct ones exertion to produce a product or perform a service and exchange that produce or service, in competition with others, in a free market, in the absence of government restriction against any activity that is not directly restricted by the people themselves in open referendum."*

*Merrill Jenkins Sr.*

The author does not choose to use the term Capitalism as a type of economic system. He prefers the terms Free Trade, Free Market, or Free Enterprise because they represent a more accurate description of the concepts and ideas for promoting free trade, private property, and a *wealth* medium of exchange. The terms Free Trade, Free Market, and Free Enterprise were in widespread use before the word Capitalism was used to define the economic system in the West. The former term started with Adam Smith during the late 18th century, and the latter term (capitalism) started in the Karl Marx era during the late 19th century.

Capitalism is a term that was coined by Karl Marx and popularized by sociologists and historians with socialist or liberal leanings. These people were enemies of the free market, free trade, or so-called capitalist economies. They saw that private capital (wealth used to produce more wealth) was the dominant force behind economic advancement in the West and that capital could increase production much faster than labor or land. So they coined the economic system in the west as "Capitalism." They ignored the fact that *all* economies use capital to some extent, including socialist economies. And that the name could have applied to them as well.

The real test to determine if an economy is a free market or socialist is whether or not the capital is privately owned (the free market) or state-owned (socialism). The answer to this fact makes a huge difference in the efficiency and success of economic advancement and prosperity.

Western economists accepted the label of capitalism unwisely, thinking that the term clearly described the source of the great material improvements in the West. These Western economists overlooked that the real source of economic advancement was freedom, including free trade and private property, accompanied by a *wealth* medium of exchange, limited government, and individual responsibility. These are the sources of capital. Capital is not the source of them. All together, they made it possible to accumulate wealth, savings, and resulting capital.

Capital is wealth used to produce more wealth. It is a means of production. In modern times the word capital is being supplanted by the term technology. But technology is simply capital too.

The free market, including the division of labor, provides for excess production overconsumption. Savings is what is left after consumption, and these savings are the source of increased capital. The savings (wealth) could be loaned to entrepreneurs for investment in new machinery (capital), which would continue to increase production over consumption.

As a result, more savings could generate more capital, and more capital could generate wealth in abundance. As the process continues, wealth and capital become self-generating and self-perpetuating. As long as the capital is in private hands, the people can increase wealth and enjoy a higher standard of living. Thus, a more precise term to describe the market process of exchanging goods and services by competitive bidding is *free* trade, *free* enterprise, or *free* market. The keyword in this economic activity is 'free,' and it should be free and competitive for everybody. And therefore, no one would have an unfair advantage over another.

When the free trade process functions properly with the essentials of a wealth medium of exchange, limited government, private property, division of labor, and individual responsibility, savings can come forth in wealth. From the savings comes capital. Capital is *"wealth used in the form of machinery and tools in the production of more wealth."* It can be generated, grown, and multiplied.

Capital is the tools and machinery in the hands of people being applied to the natural resources on the earth to create wealth aplenty. It generates, multiplies, and sustains economic development in extraordinary dimensions. Subsequently, it plays a major part in advancing civilization and culture.

It is neither the land nor the people that accelerate wealth. It is capital in the hands of people AND applied to the land that accelerates wealth! If capital is taken away from the people and the land today, today's production levels would be about the same as they were in ancient times. The rate of population would probably increase faster than the production rate, and people could be faced with starvation and desolation.

In 1798, Thomas Robert Malthus advocated that unchecked population growth was exponential while the growth in the food supply was expected to be arithmetical. But Malthusian's theory was developed before free-market economics, capital accumulation developed, and before the industrial revolution took root. As long as labor and capital are free, the Malthusian theory will not affect human progress and will even reverse Malthus' theory. Capital and technology will generate food and material benefits way beyond the mere subsistence level.

Capital (technology) allows production to increase faster than the population. The capital, in the form of tools, machinery, and technology, is the cause of the increase in wealth and prosperity and the elimination of poverty and starvation.

A free-market economic system is essential for the uplift of humanity. It is based on the voluntary and mutual exchange of goods and services, minus coercion, force, or fraud - violence. In a free-market economy, each contract, transaction, agreement, and payment associated with them is privately determined and voluntarily accepted by all parties involved. There are no legal tender laws for the private sector in a genuinely free market.

This changes when legal tender laws are interjected into the market economy. According to the ***Second College Edition of the American Heritage Dictionary***, legal tender is ***"Currency that may be offered in payment of a debt and that a creditor must accept."*** When the government forces a particular currency (legally) on the citizens and among the citizens, it then becomes mandatory 'legal tender.' When this happens, people are no longer free to make their exchanges in wealth mutually acceptable to one another. They are *forced* to accept legal tender regardless of any previous or mutually agreed upon contract terms. In fact, all contracts among private citizens that stipulate payment in real wealth or anything other than the legal tender (paper) become void.

However, when it comes to the non-private sector and the State governments, the U.S. Constitutions say that **"no State shall…make anything but gold and silver coin a tender in payment of debts…."** This means that the fifty States should pay gold and silver coins debts and receive only gold and silver coins in payment. This will prevent people from paying taxes and fines with chickens, cows, pigs, bushels of wheat, etc., to the States. And the States should not try to pay debts to citizens in credits or fiat unredeemable paper.

The medium of exchange in a free market economy MUST be a *wealth* medium. This medium of exchange is a market, social or private citizen's phenomenon. It is not a creation of the government or the banks. It can be any form of wealth found or created anywhere, *but not from an only source*. When it comes to metals, private citizens are the ones who extract them from the earth from many and sometimes unexpected locations. Bankers and government politicians do not extract it or generate them. But they conspire together to confiscate it from the people through deception, fraud, and force. And the value of the mediums of exchange should be based on free-market forces, not government decree.

Historically, the best mediums of exchange have proven to be precious metals, represented by proxy in the marketplace with 100 percent redeemable paper currency. The paper currency must be able to redeem (on demand) the wealth (precious metals) that the paper currency represents.

Precious metals (gold, silver, copper, nickel, platinum, etc.) are the only mediums of exchange that possess all four qualities of a good medium of exchange. These qualities are durability, transportability, divisibility, and relative scarcity. A fifth quality is that it is relatively stable in value.

When a redeemable paper currency is injected into the market economy, it is not the real wealth medium of exchange. It stands proxy in the marketplace as a certificate (or receipt) in lieu of the real wealth that it represents. The paper certificate is not real wealth, but it should be able to redeem real wealth on demand to the bearer of the paper certificate (or receipt). The real wealth would be the precious metals on deposit in the storage facility, whether called a bank, depository, or vault.

It took human labor to obtain wealth in the form of precious metals, and human exertion has exchange value. Therefore, precious metals have real value and real exchange value. The value is based on the subjective value of each laborer's exertion.

Government in free-market economies is necessary when it overpowers and removes any negative forces that unjustly destroy life, liberty, property, and people's ability to exchange goods and services. It protects citizens from fraudulent activities, even by the 'pious frauds.' Government should be limited and decentralized mainly for this purpose.

Under limited government, citizens will have more freedom to manage their personal and private affairs, which they can do better than any government politician. It is the citizen's responsibility to manage their own affairs, and politicians should not try to take that away from them. If they do, the people will become dependent on them just like slaves are on their masters.

A prerequisite for this freedom requires moral responsibility and individual initiative. It requires vigilance on the part of the citizens to monitor the growth and perversions of bigger government.

A constitutional republic is the form of government best compatible with a free-market economic system. Under a constitutional republic featuring limited government, there is minimal interference, intervention, or regulation of the economy by the state. The free market is self-regulating in terms of production, distribution, and consumption, and the costs or pricing that are relative to each. The market is self-regulating in terms of supply or demand and vice versus. The proper function of government in the economy is to remove all obstacles that prevent the economy from self-regulating.

In a free-market economy, private property, private enterprise, the profit motive, and private charity are four indispensable features. Taxes are paid on real property, not on improvement. And especially not on income. Citizens are only taxed according to benefits received by them.

A few monopolies can exist in a free market, but they rarely exist for long periods of time. Monopolies that exist for any length of time in a free market do so for two main reasons. One of the reasons is fair and open market competition. This assumes a company delivers the best products or services at the lowest prices minus fraud and the absence of government interference.

Following this reasoning, the common everyday consumers (the people) place a particular company on top in a monopoly status. They do this by continually buying its products or services. The masses (or the majority) are the ones who create this particular monopoly. They vote with their "dollars," or more accurately, with their *wealth* mediums of exchange to put the enterprise on top.

The second way a company can become a monopoly and continue as a monopoly is through socialistic policies. This happens when the government interferes, intervenes, and protects a company or companies (oligopoly) from external competition, domestically or internationally. They usually protect existing businesses, or they occasionally protect new or 'up and coming' businesses from outside competitors. This makes it nearly impossible for others to compete fairly and successfully against that particular protected/established company or companies.

The free-market forces should determine all prices, wages, and rents through *"the law of competitive bidding"* with no government intervention or influence. Market forces establish prices, rents, wages, et cetera in a free market through *'competitive bidding.'* These compensations are not set by biases of government politicians, labor unions, or any other structured organization.

An *"invisible hand"* or third party or neutral party in a free market, not buyer, not seller, not the state government, and not unions, will establish wages, rents, prices, and profits or losses. The "invisible hand" and the *"law of competitive bidding"* are basically the same concepts. They represent objective and unbiased market forces that ensure fair, just, and ethical economic activities.

The free market *"law of competitive bidding"* over a period of time is objective and unbiased as to race, religion, and sex. It is "the law of competitive bidding" (and negotiations) that determine fair and just wages, rents, prices, and profits or losses. It is based upon the majority of buyers and sellers interacting voluntarily without coercion, force, fraud, or government interference.

When labor unions set prices through collective bargaining, it uses a communist principle *"from each according to his ability—to each according to his needs."*

When 'price ceilings' (meaning prices that cannot be raised by businesses higher than the arbitrarily selected ceiling set by the government) that are <u>below</u> the market price are implemented, it restricts the supply of goods and services to citizens.

These prices held *below* the market price by the government increase the artificial demand for the products and services. At the same time, it restricts their supply which results in shortages. Producers will not produce (provide) as much in quantity or quality when they are forced to receive a lesser price. As a result, the number of products and services cannot keep up with the spike in demand for them.

The new production of products and services is discouraged simply because producers know they will not get paid market value. They know that they can only make a minimum profit or no profit at all. Eventually, price controls result in rationing, cost-controls, subsidies, and universal price-fixing.

Rent controls occur when a ceiling is placed by the government on how high rents can be raised. The same principle that applies to 'price ceilings' applies to rent controls. When rent controls are incorporated, they discourage the building of new dwellings. They discourage the repair of older or existing properties. In both cases, the property owners will make less or no profit. When the property owners make less profit, they do not readily reinvest or repair their properties.

On the other hand, they usually reinvest and make necessary repairs when they make a decent profit without rent controls. Subsequently, this anti-free market policy (rent controls) creates wasteful space, run-down neighborhoods, and shortages of decent low-rent housing for the poor. In many cases, rent control (where arbitrarily set rent values are held *below* the market rent values) results in slum conditions. There is very little investment in these neighborhoods, and they deteriorate rapidly.

Wage controls work the opposite of 'price ceilings' and 'rent controls,' but they have a similar effect. Wage controls exist when a minimum (or floor wage) is arbitrarily determined by government politicians who make it illegal for an employer to pay a wage *below* the arbitrarily set minimum or floor wage. This minimum (or floor wage) is placed *higher than* the market wage for a job.

When wage controls are implemented *higher than* the market wage, employers who pay the higher wage and still try to maintain their profit margins will increase prices to the general public and lay off some of their workers. This will increase unemployment. As a result, a <u>few</u> people who receive the minimum wage will benefit at the expense of the laid-off workers and the general public (who actually subsidize the higher minimum wages).

In addition, the general public will pay higher prices for goods and services produced as an added expense for those unemployed by the layoffs; layoffs are due to a higher minimum wage for the few.

In other words, additional expenses are imposed upon the taxpayers as they are taxed to take care of the unemployed and the newly created poor through some kinds of welfare programs.

Tariffs also hurt the free market by protecting particular favored industries from domestic and world international competition. They reward the inefficient producers at the expense of the efficient ones. They help to create monopolies and oligopolies in the home country. These monopolies and oligopolies are shielded from market competition nationally and internationally.

And the worse and most complex competition comes from foreign state-owned corporations. These are financed and protected by foreign governments' power of taxation.

Tariffs increase the cost to the general public in the home country through higher prices and higher taxes.

Tariffs are just another name for taxation imposed by the home government on imported goods and mostly cheaper goods from foreign countries. They are designed to increase the cost to foreigners so that domestic manufacturers, farmers, and businesses do not have to compete equally and fairly in a free trade environment.

Tariffs foster monopolies and oligopolies for a specific special interest group, whether that group is a particular class, caste, or race. It can permanently put a privileged class, caste, or race on top of the economic ladder. And the unfortunate "others" that are not privileged or favored are put permanently on the bottom.

Tariffs make it difficult and sometimes impossible for foreign companies to compete from abroad against the protected incumbent domestic companies. Also, domestic 'start-up' companies, especially disadvantaged minority groups within the domestic or national economy find it difficult or nearly impossible to enter into a market and compete against these same protected incumbent monopolies/oligopolies.

Competitors from abroad (and at home) view tariffs as barriers to entry into various domestic industries. Tariffs raise the prices of foreign goods to domestic consumers because of the increased cost of doing business forced on foreigners. Foreigners have to cover this cost and maintain their profit margins. Therefore, they must increase their export prices, making their goods less competitive. These foreign price increases hurt domestic consumers, who pay more for both foreign and domestic goods.

Tariffs also raise the prices of domestic goods because most manufacturers and farmers who advocate tariffs on foreign goods do not keep their prices low after each new round of imposed tariff hikes. On the contrary, manufacturers, and farmers simply shift their domestic prices above, equal to, or just under the new round of increased prices caused by tariffs imposed on their foreign competitors. These domestic price increases hurt domestic consumers.

It's a game of deceit that politicians, monopolies, and oligopolies play with the domestic consumers footing the bill. The consumers pay higher and higher prices while the monopolies and oligopolies associated with manufacturing and farming get richer.

As a result of tariff hikes, harmful price increases on goods and services to domestic consumers comes from both foreign and domestic companies.

Subsidies occur when the government intervenes in the economy and provides direct (or indirect) financial support to particular private (or public) businesses to keep them from failing. Subsidies can prevent companies from failing (going bankrupt), being sold, or reorganized. It stops other, more competent owners and managers from taking over the reins and making a business profitable in open competition in a free market.

New owners may be able to make the companies profitable by cutting costs, improving management, and providing better products and services at the lowest prices for the benefit of all consumers.

Many industries receive continuous subsidies because government politicians do not want them to fail. Politicians choose to provide them with a competitive advantage. They exchange political favors for money, votes, etc. On the other hand, if the non-competitive companies were allowed to fail, other more competent individuals and companies could replace them and run the businesses more efficiently and profitably.

In nearly all cases, the products or services will still be needed by the people. Therefore, the products or services that people need could still be bought at the right price – the market price. It means that costs will be cut, and prices will fall, which benefits the consumers – the masses.

Tax laws, especially income tax, are usually arbitrary, biased, and subjective. The income tax is not based upon anything scientific, natural, or just. It allows indirect (backdoor) subsidies to private and government businesses through tax exemptions, tax rebates, tax credits, etc., all at the expense of hardworking taxpayers.

Income taxes are withheld from individuals <u>before</u> expenses and taken from businesses <u>after</u> expenses.

This is another example of how a privileged few benefit at the expense of all taxpayers in general. When individuals and businesses do not pay taxes or defer their taxes, then the differences have to be paid by others. Those 'others' are other taxpayers. This unjustly redistributes and transfers wealth from taxpayers to private and public businesses. Even when the redistributed wealth goes to public companies, it is still unjust because public companies, by nature, are unjust.

In a free market, there are three main kinds of businesses. They are sole proprietorships, partnerships, and corporations. All three are private entities in a free market economy.

Corporations are usually the largest, making it possible for anybody, including the 'little man,' to participate in business ownership. This is done through the purchase of stocks and bonds in a particular corporation.

Sole Proprietorships are usually owned and operated by a single person or family.

A Partnership is simply two or more people coming together to be business partners.

There would be no government or state-owned businesses competing with private businesses in a free market. This would create a huge disadvantage for private companies regardless of their kind. To compete successfully, private concerns will have to rely on their 'good will' and quality products or services sold at the lowest prices. They must keep costs as low as possible, or they will find themselves out of business. Private businesses will simply not make enough profits to survive if they have to compete with government or state businesses while at the same time sacrificing their profits to pay taxes to support competing government businesses.

On the other hand, government or State businesses do not have to worry about profits or losses in the same way as private businesses. Suppose the government or state businesses offer inferior products or services and incur losses. In that case, all the government (owner) has to do is increase taxes to supplement its losses, continue in business, and eventually drive its private competitors out of business.

Eventually, the government or state-supported businesses will be the only ones left standing, having established a *state monopoly* in business. Therefore, government or state businesses on any level (federal, state, local) will sabotage a *true* free-market economy.

Foreign governments or nations should not be allowed to invest or compete in a private free market for the same reason. Domestic and foreign private businesses will have an unfair advantage because the citizens in their respective foreign countries will be forced by unfair taxation to subsidize the foreign government's losses. While at the same time, they continue to compete with domestic and foreign private businesses.

Only foreign *private* investors and enterprises, competing on an equal basis against other domestic and private concerns, should be allowed to establish businesses in a free market. But the private companies in a truly free market have no government support— regulatory or financial. And that is the way it's supposed to be.

With no artificial barriers to entry, employers face stiff competition in a free market every single day. If there are no artificial barriers to entry, they will be forced to hire the best workers regardless of race, religion, class, caste, or tribe to increase their profits and survive in business. This is why the free market is an economic system that works to destroy racism, class consciousness, caste, and tribalism.

On the other hand, if they (employers) are foolish enough to insist on a hiring policy based upon a particular race, sex, class, or for any reason other than the best productive worker, competition will force them entirely out of business.

When it comes to the concept of division of labor, it is indisputable that human beings have diverse abilities, talents, and skills. They apply their respective abilities, talents, and skills to natural resources using capital to produce wealth. These resources are not distributed evenly throughout the earth. No one person, group, or nation can be by its lonesome self-sufficient enough in all that is needed for optimal survival.

Cooperation is essential when people specialize in what they are best suited to satisfy the needs of others (which will allow them to get what they need). This natural and voluntary arrangement causes people to cooperate, establish peaceful relationships, and subsequently advance civilization.

The division of labor increases wealth for individuals (and nations of individuals) because everyone specializes in what they do best. They produce more when they have a specialized skill than when they only have a general or surface knowledge about a lot of different things. As people discover their life's purpose and passion and specialize in them respectively, they become more productive and peaceful (within and without).

No lone individual can produce all that they need and want beyond a subsistence level. Because of the division of labor or specialization of labor, individuals cooperate to produce products and services in greater quantities than what they need. This cooperation is essential and works to distribute or redistribute wealth more equitably and justly.

The *opposite* of the division of labor can be seen in the man skilled in writing and education but tries to be self-sufficient by building his own house, supplying his own food, being his own plumber, electrician, doctor, mechanic, painter, tailor, barber, etc. If he tries to be a successful quality producer and performer in everything he does, he won't be very successful in any of them because of time and talent constraints. He is trying to be a 'jack-of-all-trades,' but he will never be a master of any. His standard of living will rapidly retrogress back to a primitive level of existence.

Regardless of how intelligent people are, they will live in poverty and misery if they do not engage in labor specialization and maintain the right to voluntary exchanges of their surplus goods with others (through cooperation and without coercion). A person may have the potential to do anything, but it is a fact that he can never do everything.

When individuals or groups trade with each other through voluntary exchanges, they seldom fight and make war. When nations freely trade with one another and goods cross borders on both sides, armies tend not to do so. They become interdependent to the point that when one party hurts the other, they also hurt themselves.

Although the free market is known for its competitive nature, *cooperation* is more dominant. People actually compete to cooperate. Without cooperation, nothing can get done. The creation of wealth involves a higher form of competition which requires cooperation. A person can compete through cooperation for things that already exist, or he can compete by way of collaboration to make something new that does not already exist.

It is possible to compete to create. But cooperation is always needed. For instance, when two sports teams compete, they create a new result. It matters not who was the winner in the past or who won a championship the prior year. They cooperate to compete to create a new winner or new champion – a new result. The same is with businesses; they compete to create a new result every day, every year. Both competition and cooperation lead to creation becoming endless and unlimited.

A free market is characterized by a small rich class, a very large middle class, and a small poor class. However, there is an opportunity for vertical mobility. The potential to move up and down between classes is much easier as compared to other economic systems. The poor can become rich, and the rich can become poor. And in most cases, either can become middle class.

*"The system of free enterprise has been dubbed capitalism in order to deprecate and to smear it."*

**Ludwig Von Mises, "Human Action"**

*"Socialists look upon people in the same manner that the gardener views his trees. Just as the gardener capriciously shapes the trees into pyramids, parasols, cubes, vases, fans, and other forms, so does the socialist whimsically shape human beings into groups, series, centers, sub-centers, honeycombs, labor-corps, and other variations. And just as the gardener needs axes, pruning hooks, saws, and shears to shape his trees, so does the socialist need the force that he can find only in law to shape human beings. For this purpose, he devises tariff laws, tax laws, relief laws, and school laws.*

*"Socialists look upon people as raw material to be formed into social combinations…*

*"In the same manner, an inventor makes a model before he constructs the full-sized machine; the chemist wastes some chemicals — the farmer wastes some seeds and land — to try out an idea.*

*"But what a difference there is between the gardener and his trees, between the inventor and his machine, between the chemist and his elements, between the farmer and his seeds! And in all sincerity, the socialist thinks that there is the same difference between him and mankind!*

*"They look upon society as an artificial creation of the legislator's genius. This idea… has taken possession of all the intellectuals and famous writers of our country. To these intellectuals and writers, the relationship between persons and the legislator appears to be the same as the relationship between the clay and the potter.*

*"Moreover, even where they have consented to recognize a principle of action in the heart of man — and a principle of discernment in man's intellect — they have considered these gifts from God to be fatal gifts. They have thought that persons, under the impulse of these two gifts, would fatally tend to ruin themselves. They assume that if the legislators left persons free to follow their own inclinations, they would arrive at atheism instead of religion, ignorance instead of knowledge, poverty instead of production and exchange."*

*"According to these writers, it is indeed fortunate that Heaven has bestowed upon certain men — governors and legislators — the exact opposite inclinations, not only for their own sake but also for the sake of the rest of the world! While mankind tends toward evil, the legislators yearn for good; while mankind advances toward darkness, the legislators aspire for enlightenment; while mankind is drawn toward vice, the legislators are attracted toward virtue. Since they have decided that this is the true state of affairs, they then demand the use of force in order to substitute their own inclinations for those of the human race.*

*"Open at random any book on philosophy, politics, or history, and you will probably see how deeply rooted in our country is this idea — the child of classical studies, the mother of socialism. In all of them, you will probably find this idea that mankind is merely inert matter, receiving life, organization, morality, and prosperity from the power of the state. And even worse, it will be stated that mankind tends toward degeneration, and is stopped from this downward course only by the mysterious hand of the legislator. Conventional classical thought everywhere says that behind passive society there is a concealed power called law or legislator (or called by some other terminology that designates some unnamed*

*person or persons of undisputed influence and authority)
which moves, controls, benefits, and improves mankind.*

*"He who would dare to undertake the political creation of a
people ought to believe that he can, in a manner of speaking,
transform human nature; transform each individual — who,
by himself, is a solitary and perfect whole — into a mere part
of a greater whole from which the individual will henceforth
receive his life and being. Thus the person who would undertake
the political creation of a people should believe in his ability to
alter man's constitution; to strengthen it; to substitute for the
physical and independent existence received from nature, an
existence which is partial and moral. In short, the would-be
creator of political man must remove man's own forces and
endow him with others that are naturally alien to him."*

Frederic Bastiat, "The Law"

# *Greed vs Covetousness*

## "At the heart of Socialism is Covetousness"

In common language, both terms (greed and covetousness) are used interchangeably because of blurred definitions that project the same meaning. And many times, they project the same mistrust and disgust.

From ancient times in secular literature and present-day translations or interpretations of scriptural revelation transcripts, they (greed and covetousness) have lost their true meaning and intent. They have lost their differences. But there is a subtle and significant difference. And that the differences can have almost opposite effects in terms of human progress.

Napoleon Hill said, "the starting point of all achievement is desire." Greed is having a strong excessive desire for something - good or bad. It has been turned into a bad word, just like the word profit. And profit is simply *"the wealth production in excess of consumption during successful efforts of capital and labor."* Just like greed, it motivates individuals to improve themselves and work for noble causes. When the intent is right, greed is good! When you add legitimate competition and cooperation, it makes civilizations advance. It is similar to having dreams and ambitions. It motivates people to learn skills, get educated, and work hard. Because they want more than what they have, individuals seek improvement from day to day and year to year.

As long as they do not destroy, in the process, anyone else's life, liberty, or property, individuals are free to follow their own "pursuits of happiness." It makes them better, and as a result, it makes society better.

Covetousness is desiring something (or someone) that does not belong to an individual but to someone else. It is like wanting something a person did not earn or work for, which will worsen the individual and society. Covetousness is always evil!

Covetousness is a man not wanting a wife like his neighbor, but it is him wanting/ desiring his neighbor's actual wife. It is not him wanting a house or car like his neighbor, but wanting/desiring his neighbor's actual house and his actual car. It is not wanting a home or savings account like his neighbor but wanting/desiring his neighbor's actual home or savings account.

It will cause jealousy and envy, and all of the deadly sins.

Covetousness will break many of the Ten Commandments, such as do not commit adultery, do not steal, do not bear false witness, do not kill, do not disbelieve (worship other gods or no God at all, worship idols, vain self-worship, take God's name in vain, not keeping the Sabbath day, and not honoring one's parents). It is placed as the last of the Ten Commandments as an underpinning for the others.

The truth is trapped in incorrect and false definitions. Once people are free from being trapped in these two blurred meanings or misunderstood words, they will become saner, and the world will become a better place. But when they try to cover themselves with self-righteous pretentious morality, they compromise and capitulate, trying to avoid extremes. They try to find the middle ground but end up sacrificing lifesaving principles. They unwittingly strive for and settle for mediocrity.

Being extreme is not good except when seeking freedom, justice, equal opportunity, and optimal survival. Striving for truth, righteousness, and excellence are all pro-survival thoughts and behaviors. They require much dedication and intensity and can cover a lifetime.

In today's world, people are accusing other people of being greedy. On the other hand, some people accuse others of being covetous. The world is divided into two ideological camps in the political world and political parties. One 'non - wealth building' group calls another group greedy because it desires to create wealth. And the 'wealth building' group is calling the other group covetous because it wants to confiscate wealth and redistribute it to someone who did not earn it or to whom it does not belong.

So, we must ask ourselves, are we on the side of greed or covetousness?

Will we be trapped in language, or will we be free?

*"I have never understood why it is "greed" to want to keep the money you have earned but not greed to want to take somebody else's money."*

*Thomas Sowell*

# Chapter 9

# *Socialism in General*

**"Socialism, like the ancient ideas from which
it springs, confuses the distinction between
government and society. As a result of this,
every time we object to a thing being done by
government, the socialists conclude that we object
to its being done at all."**

**Frederic Bastiat, "The Law"**

Socialists want governments to nationalize big businesses or control them through regulations. They also advocate government control by supporting and financing big companies for the benefit of the laborers. This leads to the government monopoly of big business and the government monopoly of big labor through unionization.

At the same time, it opens the door for big businesses and big labor to sway tremendous power and influence over government politicians. Also, the socialists want big companies to support the citizens through the government taxation of big businesses. They never consider that the government should stay completely out of the loop and allow businesses to check one another by competing with each other for the consumer's monies and the best laborers.

This way, taxpayers can keep more of their own money to support themselves from the start. After all, each 'dollar' going to the government by way of taxation comes back much less in value to those who originally sent the 'dollars' (taxes) to the government in the first place. This is true, especially after going through the hands of politicians, government bureaucracies, and all kinds of red tape.

Socialists never consider letting big businesses support and finance themselves through stocks and bond issues and striving and surviving in open market competition. No, they want to see big companies nationalized. They want all major enterprises to be state-owned and operated.

However, it is only in the open free market that businesses will have the freedom and opportunity to succeed if they can and fail if they must, with no government assistance or control either way. The Businesses' success will depend upon them providing the best products and services at the lowest affordable prices.

It can only be assumed that socialists do not believe the masses of people are intelligent enough to manage their personal affairs. They think no one should have to worry about providing their own food, clothing, housing, retirement, or medical care. When the masses of people accept this way of thinking, it is a classic manifestation of a prison mentality. The people in prison do not have to worry about those things either. For this reason, many of them continue to go back and become institutionalized (socialized). Many retire in the system. However, they have to give up their freedoms to get these creature comforts.

In a socialist society, it is the same way. People are not free! They only eat the food that the government gives them. They pick from the clothes that the government allows them to have. They live in government houses and receive only the government's medicine. They do this for their entire lives, even in their retirement years. And just like the prisoners, they cannot come and go as they please, work in careers of their choice, or go to a school where they want. Every day people cannot read, watch the news, or listen to what they want when they want. The everyday citizens cannot travel within their own country or go abroad as they please. That is why some people see prisons as *slavery by another name.*

Without freedom, nothing is left but slavery, suffering, and death. If being a prisoner is not exactly a slave (who works for free), then it is close. It is distinguished only by the fact that an enslaved person works for free and involuntarily. But a prisoner is one who commits a criminal act and is found guilty in a court of law by his peers with due process of law. It can only be assumed that the socialists think the masses are stupid and criminal-minded and that government politicians know what is best for them.

Nevertheless, we see over and over in society those who want to shed the burden of responsibility:

> *"Millions of citizens are doing all with their power to rid themselves of responsibility for self as if it were a dreaded burden. They implore government to be responsible for their prosperity, their welfare, their security, even their children. They voluntarily drift – nay, militantly march- toward total irresponsibility.*

> *"And on the other side of the coin are the governmental power seekers – all too ready to accommodate. Members of the hierarchy who devoutly wish to assume responsibility for the people's lives and livelihoods – with the people's money! – are greeted less with resistance than with eager acceptance. Laws are then written to enforce compliance; that is, government forcibly takes the responsibility for problems, as much from those who oppose as from those who applaud the transfer of responsibility.*

> *"Together – those who eagerly shed responsibility and those who as avidly assume it for others – they present not only a collapse of self but a landslide to tyranny.*

***"Strikes, riots, and other provocative demonstrations are but the actions of a people bereft of self-respect."***

**Frederic Bastiat, "The Law"**

Many economic systems fall under the label of socialism. These systems differ only in name and by the degree of government control. They all practice government intervention in the economy. We call them economic systems, but the more government intervenes and controls them, the more impossible it is to recognize them as true economic systems.

Under socialism, economics takes a back seat to politics. In reality, they are nothing but political systems based upon decrees, edicts, executive orders/privileges, or legislation. Many of the more popular labels or 'shades of socialism' will be explained in this chapter. Some are feudalism, mercantilism, fascism, and Nazism, including socialism proper. Their various labels will identify other shades of socialism.

Again, it is essential to realize that socialism is not considered an economic system only. It is as much a governmental and politically managed system. It usually falls under the monarchic or oligarchic form of government. Advocates of socialism know this. They strategically present it as an economic system opposed to 'capitalism' only.

The proponents of socialism strategically attach themselves to a mainstream political party. Then they deceptively introduce and incorporate socialist policies into a free society through political and legislative tactics. They never use the word socialism for fear of 'blowing their cover,' but they use terminology like wealth redistribution, regulation, subsidy, bailout, etc. They rarely publicly call themselves socialists at all when supporting a mainstream political party. They simply advocate for legislation that aligns with socialist principles and policies.

Most people who do not know the difference between socialism and a free market are unaware that they support politicians who support the overthrow of the free market, limited government, and personal responsibility – and their own freedom!

The path to ignorance, poverty, and socialism can be summed up in the following statement by Plato:

> *"The greatest principle of all is that nobody, whether male or female, should be without a leader. Nor should the mind of anybody be habituated to letting him do anything at all on his own initiative; neither out of zeal, nor even playfully. But in war and in the midst of peace – to his leader he shall direct his eye and follow him faithfully. And even in the smallest matter he should stand under leadership. For example, he should get up, or move, or wash, or take his meals...only if he has been told to do so. In a word, he should teach his soul, by long habit, never to dream of acting independently, and to become utterly incapable of it."*

# Chapter 10

# *Feudalism (SOCIALISM)*

*"But how is this legal plunder to be identified?
Quite simply. See if the law takes from some
persons what belongs to them and gives it to other
persons to whom it does not belong. See if the law
benefits one citizen at the expense of another by
doing what the citizen himself cannot do without
committing a crime.*

*"Then abolish this law without delay, for it is not
only an evil itself, but also it is a fertile source for
further evils because it invites reprisals. If such
a law — which may be an isolated case — is not
abolished immediately, it will spread, multiply,
and develop into a system.*

*"The person who profits from this law will
complain bitterly, defending his acquired rights.
He will claim that the state is obligated to protect
and encourage his particular industry; that this
procedure enriches the state because the protected
industry is thus able to spend more and to pay
higher wages to the poor working men.*

*"Do not listen to this sophistry by vested interests.
The acceptance of these arguments will build
legal plunder into a whole system. "In fact, this
has already occurred. The present-day delusion
is an attempt to enrich everyone at the expense of*

*everyone else; to make plunder universal under the pretense of organizing it."*

*Frederic Bastiat, "The Law"*

The Feudal system represented a historical legacy of government ownership and control of the land and people through a king, ruler, or leader functioning as the executor, legislator, and judge. Under feudalism, people were owned and controlled by barons and lords who got their rights and titles directly from the king. This custom of government ownership and control of the land, labor (people), and resources was classic socialism/communism. Socialism/communism is nothing new, for it is the same old economic structure that sprouted from ancient times under feudalism.

Socialists want to argue that feudalism and free-market capitalism are similar and that (in either case) workers are exploited. This is not true. They fail to understand that feudalism and socialism are the same; they both own and exploit workers. The comparison is not between feudalism and capitalism, but it is between feudalism/ socialism vs. capitalism. And the choice must be between feudalism/ socialism vs. capitalism.

Under a free market system, workers own themselves (they are free). They can work for other employers/capitalists, or they can work for themselves. Workers can also own land and choose where to buy the land and live. They can generate savings and capital for themselves.

Feudalism was the *domestic* economic situation *before* mercantilism expanded it to the level of an international economic system under imperialistic political control. The feudal system was domestic and had indigenous people called serfs doing the labor. Under the feudal system, the king or feudal lords were the law or protectors.

Feudalism (Socialism)

The mercantilist system was international. It established overseas colonies wherein enslaved people (or other cheap laborers) worked. The emperors or kings used armies and soldiers to conquer other countries to benefit the mercantilists, also known as merchants.

Under free-market enterprise, a.k.a capitalism, the (representative) government is the law or protector for the whole society, not just the 'capitalists.' The state is the law, not the capitalists, and they are separate from one another. Feudalism and mercantilism are closer to socialism and communism than they are to any free market. They are just shades of socialism or different styles of socialism. They both oppose the free market economy.

*"...it is claimed that persons are nothing but raw material.
It is not for them to will their own improvement; they are
incapable of it...only the legislator is capable of doing this.
Persons are merely to be what the legislator wills them to
be....The legislator begins by decreeing the end for which the
commonwealth has come into being. Once this is determined,
the government has only to direct the physical and moral
forces of the nation toward that end. Meanwhile, the
inhabitants of the nation are to remain completely passive...
the people should have no prejudices, no affections, and
no desires except those authorized by the legislator."*

*"Usually, however, these gentlemen — the reformers, the
legislators, and the writers on public affairs — do not desire
to impose direct despotism upon mankind. Oh no, they are too
moderate and philanthropic for such direct action. Instead,
they turn to the law for this despotism, this absolutism,
this omnipotence. They desire only to make the laws."*

Frederic Bastiat, "The Law"

# Chapter 11

# *Mercantilism (Socialism)*

*"....it is not strange that... the human race
was regarded as inert matter, ready to receive
everything — form, face, energy, movement,
life — from a great prince or a great legislator
or a great genius... nourished on the study of
antiquity. And antiquity presents everywhere — in
Egypt, Persia, Greece, Rome — the spectacle of
a few men molding mankind according to their
whims, thanks to the prestige of force and of
fraud. But this does not prove that this situation
is desirable. It proves only that since men and
society are capable of improvement, it is naturally
to be expected that error, ignorance, despotism,
slavery, and superstition should be greatest
towards the origins of history.*

*"Today, the admirers of antiquity are not in
error when they found ancient institutions to
be such, but they are in error when they offered
them for the admiration and imitation of future
generations. Uncritical and childish conformists,
they take for granted the grandeur, dignity,
morality, and happiness of the artificial societies
of the ancient world. They do not understand that
knowledge appears and grows with the passage
of time; and that in proportion to this growth of*

***knowledge*, might *takes the side of* right, *and society regains possession of itself."***

*Frederic Bastiat, "The Law"*

In a free-market economy, a constitutionally limited government is necessary, and the goal is voluntary free enterprise domestically and free trade internationally. Imperialistic or monarchial forms of government will foster feudalism domestically and mercantilism internationally. In a mercantilist economy, a totalitarian system is needed. There will be expansive government intervention with a vast military-industrial complex presence.

Mercantilism and Imperialism will lead to direct colonialism or indirect neo-colonialism. This three-headed monster will lead to the slave trade, slavery, occupation, and oppression. Sometimes race, religion, and culture undercurrents will be used as an excuse to invade and conquer other countries for their natural resources. But the real reason is economic mercantilism for raw materials.

Beware! A constitutionally limited government and free-market economy can be transformed into an Imperialistic-mercantilist-colonial system. This usually is done through deception, propaganda, conspiracy, and violent revolutionized forces.

With all the governmental controls, regulations, and ownership, Mercantilism is another variation of a socialist economic system. State-sponsored mercantilism is an extension or expansion of domestic Feudalism projected onto the international market. Mercantilism was the economic system established by Great Britain and other European nations. It *preceded* the free market economic system. It also preceded socialism in name but not in its features. State-sponsored mercantilism was nominally destroyed in the West by the American Revolution, Adam Smith's classic - ***The Wealth of Nations***, and the subsequent emergence of the free market.

However, in reality, mercantilism did not wholly die. It survived and spread throughout Africa, Asia, and the Middle East. Mercantilism metamorphosed its evil into modern-day socialism. It is simply another shade of what is today commonly called socialism. Both systems advocate government intervention and regulation of the economy as a necessity. Both systems are spread beyond their respective domestic borders to other countries by force.

*Mercantilist (socialist) economics is the economic system that created the western slave trade and western slavery. It worked in conjunction with imperialism (which was its political counterpart) and colonialism (conquered territories - colonies). Only the free market can destroy all three.*

Mercantilism *preceded* free-market economics in the West. Now it is *succeeding* the same free-market system with a different label—neo-mercantilism, which is more popularly known as a variation of socialism! Therefore, the socialism of today and mercantilism of the past have merged to form a new economic system called neo-mercantilism.

Leaders in stronger countries must understand that it is acceptable to be globally free marketers and traders who actually <u>trade</u> with other nations. However, it is unacceptable to be mercantilists conquering other countries militarily, confiscating foreign lands, and colonizing them. They should not rob weaker countries of the lion's share of their resources and then give them back crumbs in the form of aid or charity.

Neo-mercantilism is nothing more than mercantilism of the past, plus scientific Marxism of today intertwined. It is taught in Western universities under the academic disciplines of 'political economy' or 'macroeconomics,' which are nothing more than pseudo-economic theories.

Macroeconomics is an attempt by politicians to sabotage the naturally self-regulating free market economy through man-made legislation and regulations.

During the mercantilist period, European nations colonized the West Indies, the American continent (including the 13 colonies), and other western countries and islands. The colonies could only sell their raw products to their respective 'mother country.' The mother country, of course, was the colonizing nation.

On the other hand, the colonies could only purchase products (finished or manufactured goods) from the mother country or the foreign commodities that were first routed through the mother country.

Under mercantilism, inter-colonial trade was restricted. Manufacturing was discouraged and usually forbidden within the colonies themselves. Manufacturing was done mainly in the mother country. Colonies could only use ships built in the mother country to transport their goods in the form of raw materials.

Another feature of mercantilism was that banks were not allowed to be established in the colonies. Colonies could only use 'money' (for legal tender) that the mother country issued. Taxation without representation was the norm including in the American colonies. This was one of the major grievances that led to the Revolutionary War. Mercantilism was a state-run economy, and the monarchy granted monopolies to whom it pleased.

Mercantilism is associated with corporate monopolies because it depends so heavily on them. Monopolies not only included factories but shipping and trading companies as well. Mercantilism also depended on slavery (free and cheap unskilled labor) in the colonies to produce the raw materials that were shipped directly to the monopolistic factories located within the mother country.

In the colonies, slaves provided raw labor in agriculture and crafts, not manufacturing. Manufacturing was done in the mother countries, which is why the slave trade existed so strongly in the West Indies and the American continent.

At the end of the American Revolutionary War, the American colonies were the first to officially abolish slavery in the western world (maybe in the world as a whole), starting with the newly formed state of Vermont in America in 1777. And the new U.S. Constitution (1787) called for abolishing the slave trade 20 years after its adoption.

After the American Revolution and independence from Great Britain, the triangular trade was broken. It had been forced upon the British colonies through the Navigational Laws (1651). Americans immediately began to trade with France and other nations.

What is known as 'free trade' emerged. Without the effectiveness of protectionism and subsidies to support high prices, the British West Indies' products could not compete in the emerging free trade markets. Subsequently, slavery was no longer profitable, and the West Indies' economy collapsed. Slave labor was no longer needed in the British West Indies; soon after that, the British slave trade was abolished (1807). Later, in 1834 slavery was abolished by Great Britain in the West Indies. This was only the beginning. Most other European nations did not abolish the slave trade or slavery until decades after Great Britain.

The slave trade also was abolished (per the U.S. Constitution of 1787 to become effective 20 years later). The United States actually abolished the slave trade the same year that Great Britain abolished it in 1807. But it did not become effective in America until January 1st of the following year (1808). Slavery had been partially abolished in America ever since 1777. But it was not abolished legally for all law-abiding Americans in the United States until the ratification of the 13th Amendment on December 6, 1865.

Mercantilism was in direct conflict with free-trade or laissez-faire economics. It could not survive in a free trade environment, particularly after Adam Smith's book, *The Wealth of Nations* and the American Revolution. Therefore, after the destruction of mercantilism in the West and the emergence of the free market economy, state-sponsored mercantilists turned to Africa, Asia, and the Middle East, where there was no free trade. It began to apply its same mercantilist principles to those continents and countries—mercantilism, imperialism, and colonialism were revived! Raw natural resources were expropriated with cheap unskilled labor.

Ironically, direct slavery was not a component of the mercantilism (economy) and imperialism (political) systems in African, Asian, and Middle Eastern countries. Mercantilists were effective in those areas because free trade and free enterprise had not developed very strongly in those places at the time. This made it easier for mercantilists to colonize them for nearly a hundred years. They extracted these countries' wealth (raw materials) as they had in the American West. But cheap labor was business as usual.

In fact, the European imperialist countries led by the British stamped out direct slavery among the indigenous peoples in African, Asian, and Middle Eastern countries. According to Economist Thomas Sowell, ***"Not only were Britons forbidden to trade or hold slaves, the British navy intercepted slave ships from other nations on the high seas, set the slaves free and confiscated the ships."*** It took Great Britain and other European nations nearly a hundred years, but they eventually abolished slavery in all European and non-European countries worldwide.

The European Christians were the leading slave traders in the 18th century. However, they became the leading destroyers of slavery in the 19th century (around the globe) - involving land and people. No other race led the way for its annihilation any better. Other non-European leaders around the world were pressured and forced by Europeans to end the slave trade and slavery within their own respective countries.

Slavery has been practiced since the recorded history of man. It existed for thousands of years, even before the advent of the great religions with Abrahamic roots - Judaism, Christianity, and Islam. However, those of European descent led by Great Britain, France, and America destroyed it in a little over one hundred years. Black

Americans need to take note of this historical fact since they had been mired in the worst kind of slavery when this anti-slavery movement began. This was no small achievement.

Imperialism was the foreign political policy of European nations, and Mercantilism was the economic philosophy of these conquering nations. The emergence of free-market economics (voluntary, mutual, or reciprocal trade *within* separate countries and *among* private individuals in foreign nations) did not root out mercantilism completely. A remnant remained. And that remnant re-rooted and grew elsewhere.

Today, it has returned to the West in the form of state-sponsored entitlements, government-sponsored monopolies, protectionism, tariffs, and foreign policies that attempt to control the economies of other weaker nations through wars and the threat of war. The only way mercantilism has resurfaced and survived is because the truth of its evil has been hidden due to a corrupt economic scheme of a fractional reserve monetary system and corrupt politicians.

State-sponsored mercantilism's features were many. One of them was slavery and slave trading in the West and cheap labor in Africa, Asia, and the Middle East. Slavery was a major result of mercantilism in the West, and it was introduced in the West by imperialist politics and mercantilist economics.

Colonies were founded by nations (mother countries) that conquered other lands to have what they called independent sources of natural resources.

They used slave labor to extract the raw materials and transfer them to the mother country, manufacturing them into finished goods. These conquering nations would rather practice this system than engage in mutual trade or exchange raw and finished goods with other nations.

Another feature of mercantilism emphasized exports over imports from the point of view of the mother country. Only exports of finished products were considered good, and imports (except for raw materials) from colonies were deemed to be bad. Trade surpluses were good, and deficits were bad.

This idea grew out of the bullion theory. Bullionism is the notion that wealth consists of precious metals (particularly gold) and that the value of everything else is derived from the fact that precious metals could be exchanged for it. Gold was the most universally acceptable wealth medium of exchange in the East and West. As a commodity, it hardly deteriorates; it weighs little in proportion to its exchange value for all other things. It has many practical uses, and it is malleable. It is divisible, and it is rare. As a metal, all these qualities never change. And silver is the same way.

According to this concept, prosperity depended specifically on increases in gold and silver for the State, not necessarily the general increase in wealth in products and goods for the individual citizen.

Trade became a contest among nations with the whole idea of winners and losers. Trade was used as a means of increasing the bullion holdings of nations. This was done successfully or allegedly through a favorable trade balance. *A favorable trade balance is said to exist when the goods and services that one nation sells to another exceed those bought from the other. A nation had a favorable balance of trade when exports exceeded imports.*

This was thought to be favorable because the difference would be made up of gold, and the wealth (gold) of the nation thus favored would be increased. A government that imported more than it exported would have an unfavorable trade balance, and that is because they would have to make up the difference in gold going out.

Government control, intervention, or regulation were essential under mercantilism. For example, Great Britain restricted its colonies by imposing Navigational Acts. A series of these acts were passed from 1651 through 1663. The Navigation Act of 1660 – reenacted in 1661 – required all trade with the colonies to be carried in English-built ships and manned predominantly by Englishmen. All foreign merchants were excluded from the commerce of the English colonies. Selected (listed) products or crops, e.g., tobacco, could be exported from the colonies only to Britain or other colonies under British possession.

The Staple Act (1663) provided that goods exported from European countries to English colonies must first be shipped to England. Another Navigational Act (1699) was the Woolens Act. It was an attempt to prevent certain kinds of manufacturing and trade from developing in the colonies. This act *prohibited exporting wool or woolen goods from a colony to other colonies or countries.*

The Hat Act (1732) prohibited the exportation of hats from the colony in which they were made to countries other than the mother country. It limited the number of apprentices a hatmaker might have. The Molasses Act of 1733 placed high duties on molasses, sugar, and rum imported into the colonies from any source other than British colonies. The Iron Act of 1750 permitted pig iron to be exported from the colonies to England duty-free. However, it prohibited the establishment of new iron mills from finishing products in the colonies.

Mercantilism, also known as *Economic Nationalism,* was very strong. European nations and their respective colonies competed against one another for hegemony. It usually resulted in wars and threats of war. The First Anglo-Dutch War of 1652 – 54, the Second Anglo-Dutch War of 1664, and the war between the English and the Dutch (started in 1672) were all attributed to mercantilism. This third war was why the Dutch lost power in America, and New Amsterdam was renamed New York.

The 'King William's War' of the 1690s was fought to maintain the balance of power in Europe. From 1702-1713 the 'Queen Anne's War' (or the War of the Spanish Succession) was fought to determine who would control the Americas. As a result of this war, the British gained Newfoundland, Acadia, and the Hudson Bay territory. The

'War of Jenkins Ear' (1739) was a fight over who would possess Georgia.

The War of the Austrian Succession occurred between 1740 and 1748. In 1754 the 'French and Indian War' started in America, and it would determine control of western Pennsylvania. This war extended to Europe in 1756 and became known as the 'Seven Years War.'

After a major battle won by the British at the Battle of Quebec in 1759, the 'Treaty of Paris' (1763) allowed the British to gain all the French-Canadian holdings and the French and Spanish territory east of the Mississippi. This area east of the Mississippi river contained the Northwest Territory and the Southwest Territory, and these territories were added to the 13 colonies after the defeat of England in the Revolutionary War.

As mentioned above, monopolies were an essential feature of mercantilism. The kings usually granted them through a governmental contract or grant procedure. They also were created by tariffs which were another form of government intervention. Tariffs were used as a means for revenue and protectionism, and tariffs as a tax on imported goods generated revenue. Foreign goods became more expensive and less competitive with domestic goods.

This resulted in protection (for domestic companies) from open and fair competition with foreign companies. Consequently, domestic companies became more prominent and more robust at the expense of the general public, who had to pay higher prices to foreign companies for goods and services (making them less competitive with domestics). The general public again paid higher prices to (later) domestic companies once they gained monopoly status with their goods and services.

These domestic companies became monopolistic or oligopolistic. What can be said of tariffs in the past can also be said of them today. They have the same negative monopolistic effect.

The policies of state-sponsored mercantilism are no different than those of economic **autarky** or imperialistic political **autarchy**. Autarky is defined as national independence and economic self-sufficiency. It represents an economic system that is closed to mutual trade. Autarky advocates economic self-sufficiency as a national policy. It supports getting along without imported goods from other countries – a closed economy.

Autarchy is political in nature, and it represents international imperialism. It dictates absolute rule or sovereignty by an individual, and it is synonymous with autocracy. Under autarky, the goal of nations is economic independence rather than economic interdependence. Both are motivated by a sense of national superiority and, in many cases, religious or racial superiority. Fascism, which is discussed below, also seeks to impose autarky and autarchy policies upon society.

*"Men naturally rebel against the injustice of which they are victims. Thus, when plunder is organized by law for the profit of those who make the law, all the plundered classes try somehow to enter — by peaceful or revolutionary means — into the making of laws. According to their degree of enlightenment, these plundered classes may propose one of two entirely different purposes when they attempt to attain political power: Either they may wish to stop lawful plunder, or they may wish to share in it.*

*"Woe to the nation when this latter purpose prevails among the mass victims of lawful plunder when they, in turn, seize the power to make laws! Until that happens, the few practice lawful plunder upon the many, a common practice where the right to participate in the making of law is*

*limited to a few persons. But then, participation in the making of law becomes universal. And then, men seek to balance their conflicting interests by universal plunder. Instead of rooting out the injustices found in society, they make these injustices general. As soon as the plundered classes gain political power, they establish a system of reprisals against other classes. They do not abolish legal plunder. (This objective would demand more enlightenment than they possess.) Instead, they emulate their evil predecessors by participating in this legal plunder, even though it is against their own interests.*

*"It is as if it were necessary, before a reign of justice appears, for everyone to suffer a cruel retribution — some for their evilness, and some for their lack of understanding.*

*"It is impossible to introduce into society a greater change and a greater evil than this: the conversion of the law into an instrument of plunder.*

*"...it erases from everyone's conscience the distinction between justice and injustice.*

*"When law and morality contradict each other, the citizen has the cruel alternative of either losing his moral sense or losing his respect for the law. These two evils are of equal consequence, and it would be difficult for a person to choose between them."*

Frederic Bastiat, "The Law"

# Chapter 12

# *Fascism (Socialism)*

***"The keystone of the Fascist doctrine is its
conception of the state, of its essence, its
functions, and its aims. For Fascism the state is
absolute, individuals and groups relative."***

*Benito Mussolini*

Fascism is a combined system of both economics and politics, mostly politics created by government politicians. It is characterized by a rigid one-party dictatorship, forcible suppression of all opposition, and private economic activity under centralized governmental control. Fascism is known for belligerent nationalism, racism, and militarism. It is the gateway to socialism. First, the government allows ownership of private businesses but places heavy taxes and regulations on them. Then when the companies fail, the government takes them over as socialist/government businesses.

Fascism is also classified as a mixed economy because of limited private property, private enterprise, and state economic enterprises. It functions with a one-party political system. Fascism politically is associated with a dictatorship or tyranny. Usually, the dictator or tyrant operates under the political label of monarchy and autocracy. All dissenters are destroyed. Fascism is nationalistic and oppressive, and it promotes a war-mongering agenda. Its first well-known leader was Benito Mussolini (b.1883 - d.1945). He was a ruler in Italy.

Also, fascism is characterized by centralized control of the domestic economy under a monarchic form of government. The government does not own all the means of production, distribution, and consumption, but it controls or regulates them all. It dictates what the actual private owners must do with their own properties.

The people own property in name only while the government dictates its use. Fascism is a branch of guild socialism with a different label - corporatism. Fascism has autar*ky* tendencies and advocates economic self-sufficiency as a national policy. The concept of fascism and autar*ky* promotes getting along without imports from other countries - a closed economy. Fascist economics supports the concept of strong governmental involvement. This economic system is compatible with a monarchy and oligarchic forms of government.

Under fascism, there is a small, rich class, a small middle class, and a very large poor class. There is little upward mobility from the poorer class to the middle class and from the middle class to the rich class. The rich and the elite usually maintain and perpetuate power through their bloodlines, generation after generation.

*"There is no other means of preventing social disintegration and of safeguarding the steady improvement of human conditions than those provided by reason. Men must try to think through all the problems involved up to the point beyond which a human mind cannot proceed farther. They must never acquiesce in any solutions conveyed by older generations, they must always question anew every theory and every theorem, they must never relax in their endeavors to rush away fallacies and to find the best possible cognition. They must fight error by unmasking spurious doctrines and by expounding truth."*

Ludwig Von Mises, "Human Action"

# Chapter 13

# *Nazism (Socialism)*

*"...When a portion of wealth is transferred from the person who owns it – without his consent and without compensation, and whether by force or by fraud — to anyone who does not own it, then I say that property is violated; that an act of plunder is committed.*

*"I say that this act is exactly what the law is supposed to suppress, always and everywhere. When the law itself commits this act that it is supposed to suppress, I say that plunder is still committed, and I add that from the point of view of society and welfare, this aggression against rights is even worse. In this case of legal plunder, however, the person who receives the benefits is not responsible for the act of plundering. The responsibility for this legal plunder rests with the law, the legislator, and society itself. Therein lies the political danger."*

Frederic Bastiat, "The Law"

Nazism existed as a mixed economy (some private enterprises and some government enterprises). It was nationalistic, socialistic, and extremely racist in its formation. Today, it can be classified as another variation of socialism. Its first well-known leader was Adolf Hitler (b. 1889 – d. 1945). He wrote a book on total war called **Mein Kempt**, which means "My Battle" or "My Struggle." Nazism is characterized as a dictatorial or tyrannical government with all dissenters targeted for death and destruction.

The National Socialist Labor Party (NAZI) was a one-party political system based on socialist economics and nationalism combined. One of the main features it advocated was a superior race theory. It was anti-capitalism and anti-profit. Nazism sought public or state control of the production and distribution and the redistribution of wealth. It advocated government-engineered forced income equality.

Nazis wanted to conquer larger territories rich in natural resources, allowing their nation to live in economic self-sufficiency at standards not lower than any other nation. This is a variation of mercantilism (socialism). Nazism suppressed the profit motive, which is always the prime motivator for competitive private businesses. Without coercion, the profit motive allows free-market business people to manage efficiently, lower prices, control costs and provide the best quality products and services possible.

Nazism advocated government control and management of businesses. It incorporated price ceilings and minimum wage rates. Nazis did not favor free trade, laissez-faire economics, or the gold standard. They sought an easy money policy, i.e., credit expansion. This resulted in hyperinflation and, eventually, economic collapse. They believed that importing finished goods was bad and should be discouraged. Nazis felt relying on imports made them more dependent. Their goal was national independence. Nazis believed exporting was superior to importing, making them more independent and superior. Therefore, this became their political and economic policy.

The Nazis failed to realize that trade was and will always be a 'two-way street.' In mutual trade, there is always interdependency amongst the traders. Each has something that the other wants or needs more than what they currently have. This is the cause behind mutual non-coercive economic exchanges. Otherwise, no volunteer trading would ever take place.

Eugenics was practiced under Nazism. It was an attempt to create a master race and aimed at placing some men, backed by the force of law, in complete control of human reproduction. To marry someone of an 'inferior' race was a crime.

**Nationalism + socialism + racism + violence = Nazism.** It produces men like Hitler or Hitler-like clones.

**Black Nationalism + socialism + racism + violence = the same as Nazism.** Even if it is under a different label or different race, it is still (black) Nazism. It can produce another type of Hitler with a different name and physical characteristics. Beware!!

The world is full of egomaniacs of all races with dictatorial or messianic complexes. It must be remembered that men like Mussolini and Hitler did not gain power and influence overnight. Fascism and Nazism both were the result of years, even decades, of social conditioning and propaganda directed toward the masses by socialist intellectuals. This was before they gained enough power to respectfully implement their ideas and forms of fascism and Nazism.

Under Nazism, there was a small, rich class, a small middle class, and a very large poor class. There is little upward mobility from the poorer class to the middle class and from the middle class to the wealthy class. The rich and the elite usually maintain and perpetuate power through their bloodlines, generation after generation.

*"Men must be divided into two classes: the omnipotent godlike dictator on the one hand and the masses which must surrender volition and reasoning in order to become mere chessmen in the plans of the dictator. The masses must be dehumanized in order to make one man their godlike master. Thinking and acting, the foremost characteristics of man as man, would become the privilege of one man only. There is no need to point out that such designs are unrealizable. The chiliastic empires of dictators are doomed to failure; they have never lasted longer than a few years."*

Ludwig Von Mises, "Human Action"

Chapter 14

# Socialism (Proper)

> *"Nothing can enter the public treasury for the benefit of one citizen or one class unless other citizens and other classes have been forced to send it in. If every person draws from the treasury the amount that he has put in it, it is true that the law then plunders nobody. But this procedure does nothing for the persons who have no money. It does not promote equality of income. The law can be an instrument of equalization only as it takes from some persons and gives to other persons. When the law does this, it is an instrument of plunder."*
>
> Frederic Bastiat, "The Law"

Socialism (planned chaos) is a one-party political system *imitating* an economic system. The state owns and controls major industries in a country and regulates them as it pleases. Under socialism, there is public control of the means of production. The government manages production and distribution (and redistribution) processes through a central planning authority. There is no equality in what each individual gives to or gets from the government for consumption.

Socialism is a stepping-stone to communism, and communism is the aim of socialism. They both come from the same source and advocate violent revolution as part of their strategies to establish themselves. Socialism does not propagate the principle of parliamentary government; it only knows dictatorship. Socialists regard misguided sympathizers who call themselves liberals as **"*useful idiots.*"** In a socialist society, there are few private educational systems, except for the elite. These socialist elitists always find ways to live above the masses while sending their children to the best schools, usually for free.

Other names and labels commonly used for socialism are communism, feudalism, mercantilism, neo-mercantilism, fascism, Nazism, and protectionism (against outside competition from monopolies, labor unions, special interest groups, industries, agricultural farmers, etc.).

In addition to these, other names and labels commonly used for socialism are interventionism, state capitalism, the welfare state, nanny state, state planning, communal economics, cooperative economics, collective economics, Keynesian economics, and macro-economics (which is nothing more than legislated 'economic policy'). Sometimes it is called "political economy" to erode the distinction between economic theory and political theory.

For the most part, *'legislated'* economic policy has replaced economic theory as the subject matter that is being taught in today's colleges and universities around the world. This economic policy curriculum is interventionist politics disguised as practical economics. It is based on consensus political legislation introduced by socialist politicians, not actual free-market economists.

Economic policy is not a true economic theory! Economic 'policy' is a corruption of true economic theory.' Politicians create policy and make decisions that distort the free market processes. They do this based on expediency and short-term political and personal interests. When these policies prove to be failures, politicians create even more policies to correct the failures caused by the previous bad economic policies they made before.

This process repeats until politicians and their 'economic policies control and regulates the whole economy.' This is usually the norm, and it helps neither the economy nor the masses of people in the long run. Unfortunately, when the economic policies fail, the socialists blame the bad economy on the economic theories of the free market rather than their own bad policies.

On the other hand, the real economic theory involves a market economy compatible with the natural laws of man and the universe. It reflects free human beings acting in their own best interest. Free enterprise economics is without coercion from anyone, including the government. Many diverse individuals make decisions in the marketplace seeking their own best interest, not by politicians who want to make personal decisions for them.

The free market is an economic democracy where the masses vote with their own individual "dollars" for the best products available, as the best producers supply them, and at affordable prices.

Price controls and price ceilings, rent controls and rent ceilings, wage controls (minimum wages, living wages, etc.), subsidies, tariffs, income taxes, and fractional reserve banking are all policies of socialism (political legislation).

Labor unions are the doorway to socialism. In the workplace, they practice *"from each according to his ability to each according to his need."* This is the principle in which 'collective bargaining' is spawned.

Through collective bargaining, labor unions subsidize unproductive workers at the expense of good workers. They force, on all, equal pay for what is not always equal work. Those who work the hardest get the same wages as those who don't. Labor unions condition the workers' minds to dislike (even hate) the free market and accept socialist solutions. They divide them into classes. They create separation and antagonism between workers and management/owners.

Labor unions scoff at merit pay, whereby individuals receive raises based on their respective performances. Under a pay scale based on merit pay, the hardest working and most valuable workers receive higher raises, and those who do not work as hard receive lower raises.

Under socialism, there is a small, rich class, a small middle class, and a very large poor class. There is very little upward mobility from the poorer class to the middle class and from the middle class to the rich class. The rich and the elite usually maintain and perpetuate their power through their bloodlines, generation after generation.

> ***It suffices here to say that the planned economy
> which the advocates of dictatorship wish to set
> up is precisely as socialistic as the Socialism
> propagated by the self-styled Social Democrats."***

*Ludwig von Mises*
*Socialism: An Economic and Sociological Analysis*

# Chapter 15

# *Communism (SOCIALISM)*

*"Good fortune and bad fortune, wealth and
destitution, equality and inequality, virtue and vice
— all then depend upon political administration.
It is burdened with every-thing, it undertakes
everything, it does everything; therefore it is
responsible for everything.*

*"If we are fortunate, then government has a claim
to our gratitude; but if we are unfortunate, then
government must bear the blame. For are not
our persons and property now at the disposal of
government? Is not the law omnipotent?*

*"Thus there is not a grievance in the nation for
which the government does not voluntarily make
itself responsible. Is it surprising, then, that every
failure increases the threat of another revolution?*

*"And what remedy is proposed for this? To
extend indefinitely the domain of the law; that
is, the responsibility of government. ....'The
state considers that its purpose is to enlighten, to
develop, to enlarge, to strengthen, to spiritualize,
and to sanctify the soul of the people' — and if
the government cannot do all of these things,
what then? Is it not certain that after every
government failure — which, alas, is more than*

*probable — there will be an equally inevitable revolution?"*

*Frederic Bastiat, "The Law"*

Communism, commonly interchanged with socialism as the world knows it, was founded by Karl Marx and Frederic Engels and introduced to the world in 1848 by their co-authored book titled ***The Communist Manifesto.***

This book outlines ten planks to change a free enterprise economic system over to a socialist/communist economic system and government. These ten planks are as follows:

1. ***Abolition of private property in land and application of all rents of land to public purposes.***

2. ***A heavy progressive or graduated income tax.***

3. ***Abolition of all rights of inheritance.***

4. ***Confiscation of the property of all emigrants and rebels.***

5. ***Centralization of credit in the hands of the State, by means of a national bank with state capital and an exclusive monopoly.***

6. ***Centralization of the means of communication and transport in the hands of the state.***

7. ***Extension of factories and instruments of production owned by the state, the bringing into cultivation of waste lands, and the improvement of the soil generally in accordance with a common plan.***

8. ***Equal liability of all to labor. Establishment of industrial armies, especially for agriculture.***

9. ***Combination of agriculture with manufacturing industries; gradual abolition of the distinction between town and***

*country by a more equitable distribution of population over the country.*

10. *Free education for all children in public schools. Abolition of children's factory labor in its present form. Combination of education with industrial production, etc."*

The first three planks of **<u>The Communist Manifesto</u>** seek to implement real estate taxes, including strong environmental laws, income tax, and inheritance tax. These planks coincide with communism's calls for the abolition of private property. Communists seem to have no problem taxing property/wealth away from the people or outright confiscation by force.

However, if there is no private property as advocated by communism, then there is no need for an inheritance tax because there is nothing to inherit. A steep inheritance tax is just a method used to rid the people of private property and transfer it over to government control and ownership.

The 1<u>st</u>, 2<u>nd</u>, and 3<u>rd</u> planks call for a real estate tax, an income tax, and an inheritance tax. Those who rebel against these taxes, the Communist Manifesto, and its ultimate goals *"to dethrone God, destroy 'capitalism,"* and establish a One World Government are labeled rebels. The fourth plank is "Confiscation of the property of all emigrants and rebels." Anyone who wishes to emigrate and flee from communist oppression and slavery is persecuted and made a political prisoner. Since the whole process is corrupt in the first place, the due process becomes a sham.

The fifth plank talks about state banks' exclusive monopoly in 'money' (credit) creation. The manifesto calls for this monopoly to be in the hands of the state. In the West, some private banks have a monopoly in 'money' and 'credit' creation. However, whether a monopoly by state controls or private controls, the results are practically the same as its effects on the economy. Neither state nor private monopoly banks are the proper sources for 'money' creation. 'Money' (or, more precisely, a wealth medium of exchange) creation is a social phenomenon. It should be created and controlled by the people in the marketplace through cooperative competition, eliminating any long-term monopolies.

The sixth plank of *The Communist Manifesto* calls for the control of communications, including the press, airwaves, schools and the post office, etc.

The seventh plank is to nationalize all capital (means of production) – tools, machinery, technology, and entire businesses. Whenever a government business competes in a free market with a private company, the government business has the upper hand because the government business can forever tax society to stay in business, regardless of profit and loss.

The private business is at a disadvantage because it is governed by the principle of profit and loss. If it has a loss, it can't tax anyone to fill the gap. It will eventually go out of business and leave the government business still functioning as a monopoly.

The eighth plank calls for organizing labor into a regimented-military-goose stepping workforce labeled an *"industrial army."* Compulsory unionization!

The ninth plank advocates force to abolish the distinction between city and suburbs by possibly redistributing poor people in wealthy neighborhoods. Although it is not called out specifically in the ten planks of the Communists Manifesto, communism's goal is to abolish national borders too.

The Communists Manifesto, on page 23, states: ***"The Communists are further reproached with desiring to abolish countries and nationalities. The working men have no country...."*** Communists claim that workers have no fatherland (or motherland) and no specific country. They can go wherever they please.

Illegal immigration is a political tool of Communists to destroy borders and abolish the distinction between citizens and non-citizens. This will cause disintegration and dysfunction of strong and free governments and economic systems. And it will make it easier for them to fall into the hands of the Communist and One World Government advocates, the Globalists.

A nation that cannot control its borders will lose its sovereignty, authority, and freedom.

The Communists Manifesto, in mockery, states: *"The Communists are further reproached with desiring to abolish countries and nationalities. The working men have no country...."*

Destroying borders is a communist strategy of destroying individual countries to fit in with the idea of One World Government, New World Order, or Globalism. *The working men have no country...."*

In a sovereign free country, goods can (must) cross borders, but people cannot, accept temporarily or legally, and by authorized permission. The border wall's entry and exit should be free for citizens either way. But non-citizens do not pay to exit but must pay a small fee to enter.

One fundamental cause of illegal immigration (or emigration) is that the countries where the immigrants are fleeing from do not have a Second Amendment: *"A well-regulated militia being necessary to the security of a free state, the right of the people to keep and bear arms shall not be infringed."* Dissatisfaction with one's government, immigration, or emigration can be traced back to the extent of gun control laws in the countries that are being vacated.

When the governments (in the vacated countries) are the only ones that own and control all of the guns, then the people have no defense from the oppressive or corrupt government except to flee to another country.

Other corrupt individuals/groups usually are organized criminal elements (cartels, mafia, etc.). They smuggle, own, and control all types of guns and weapons.

It gets worse when corrupt government officials and corrupt criminals merge and support one another. The average citizens are defenseless, and they are caught in the middle, severely terrorized, exploited, and reduced to poverty, suffering, and slavery.

When mass emigration is not an option, a second scenario often develops where a foreign country or countries will intervene and find (or create) another third group within the country. These foreign countries will supply the new group with arms and weapons to combat the official but corrupt government and the unofficial corrupt criminal elements.

This support by foreigners will always come with future long-term strings attached and promises of influence and control by the outside foreign government(s), provided that the group it supports is victorious.

A third scenario may develop if their group is victorious but fails to live up to its agreement with the outside forces. In this case, the victorious group will be overthrown by someone else or the foreign government(s) who will support them. Then a regime change will take place.

The fourth scenario is when the foreign government itself invades the country. Again, regime change will occur, or an indefinite occupation by an alien force will occur. This scenario falls in line with typical mercantilist philosophy. And is de facto colonization (the establishment of colonies or satellites). It matters not whether a country calls itself capitalist or communist/socialist. When it uses this philosophy, it is practicing mercantilist economics.

All this results from the indigenous citizens' inability to control and defend themselves due to gun control laws prohibiting them from owning guns and ammunition. If they could own guns for self-defense, they would eventually organize and stop political corruption, criminal terrorism, and foreign invasion.

They could establish good government and live in peace, accompanied by prosperity. They would control their government, and officials would be elected and governed by the consent of the people.

The tenth plank calls for centralized free public education for children to teach a 'standardized' script that supports the socialist-communist ideology. In the West, the public educational system supports big government, neo-mercantilism, and macroeconomics, euphemisms for socialism and communism.

Today, public education teaches Darwinism/Evolution, sex education, gay marriages, gay unions, etc. State schools forbid students from reading their own religious materials or praying to their Creator even during their free time or breaks. State control of all education destroys private independent education, not only for children but also for adults who attend colleges. It also destroys independent thinking.

The purpose of centralized government control of education is to make it easier to manipulate the minds of the youth. The purpose includes teaching propaganda and brainwashing them to think a certain way or accept a particular good or bad ideology.

Of the ten planks of *The Communist Manifesto*, America incorporated two of them in 1913 with the establishment of the Federal Reserve Banking System (plank # 5) and the graduated income tax (plank #2). The introduction of these two planks represented 20 percent of the ten planks in one single year! Public schools had already been established, but they were under local control. Today they are under federalized or centralized control, and they are failing terribly.

Since that time, America has incorporated nearly all of the ten planks of *The Communist Manifesto* into her political-economic system to some degree or another, some to a greater degree than others. And the rate and depth of these incorporations are increasing! The influence of the incorporated planks of *The Communist Manifesto* upon American society has grown widespread and deep.

And it is impacting all of America and the whole world in devastating and destructive ways.

**SOLUTION:** A communist (socialist) system can be changed back to a free market economic system by reversing the ten planks outlined in *The Communist Manifesto*. The more they are reversed, the freer the market forces will become. There will be less government involvement. People will be freer and less oppressed by the enormous number of laws abrogated. People do not fully understand most of the laws anyway. At any given moment, good upstanding citizens are breaking some obscure law and committing some dubious crime because of some petty law created by some petty politician just to feed his ego and exercise 'his' authority.

With the reverse of these ten planks, private enterprises will grow and provide more efficient products and services that society needs (based upon sound economic solutions). In addition to reversing the entire ten planks of *The Communist Manifesto,* labor unions will need to be abolished, as well as all laws protecting businesses from competing with one another on a level playing field. These two have to be eliminated together. Otherwise, their activities create artificial monopolies. They (big labor and big business) both should be abolished.

Although people (citizens) can be contained within their own national borders (except through legal immigration/emigration policies/visas, business and vacation travel via passports), there should never be any trade barriers for safe, legal goods and services crossing national borders. In other words, just as goods and services can freely crisscross state lines *within* a country, goods and services should be able to freely crisscross national borders, even if citizens are restricted from freely crossing borders for national security reasons.

And most importantly, *all legal tender laws among private citizens should be abolished!*

Communism is a one-party system. The government owns and controls all the means of production, distribution, and consumption.

This simply means total control of the people who are the producers, distributors, and consumers. The individual citizen is forbidden to own any real properties, manufacturing, businesses, etc. Under communism, the state wants to be and play God, to be feared, loved, and worshipped.

It is important to know that communism is not *only* an economic system, but it is first and foremost a political and governmental system. It normally falls either under the Monarchic or Oligarchic forms of government. Regardless of what name it uses, the central government controls the economy.

Many activists and politicians in America who advocate communism know this. They strategically present it as an economic system opposed to 'capitalism' only. But communism is opposed to both the free market and the constitutional republic (limited government) – freedom!

On the other hand, these activists and politicians deceptively introduce and incorporate it into a free society through deceptive political and legislative tactics. They never use the word communism for fear of 'blowing their cover.' They never publicly call themselves communists at all. They simply legislate communistic policies!

The majority of the people (taught in government schools) do not know the difference between communism and a free market. They are unaware that they support politicians who support communism through government legislation and regulations. The ignorant masses support politicians who want to overthrow their own government, economic system, culture, and freedom. These politicians want to replace it all with socialism/communism and slavery, whether they are being tricked into it or not.

One of the concepts advocated by communists is *"from each according to his ability, to each according to his need."* However, in reality, it is the government or state that determines one's ability and also one's needs. This concept in itself will completely destroy civilization. In this situation, the state decides what people's abilities are, then tries to force them to produce and perform to that level.

On the other hand, the state will only compensate them based upon what it (the state) decides they need, even if unsatisfied individuals believe that they need or want more in life. These individuals become slaves to the state because they are forced to go along with the state's decisions. At the same time, the people who do not produce or perform at a high level are rewarded by the state based on the state's decision that they need or deserve more than what they themselves produce.

In both cases, the tendency of human nature is *not* to produce more but less. In the first case, the people who produce more will tend to stop producing on a higher level when they are not rewarded for their effort and production. They will soon figure out that part of their products will go to the non-producers.

In the second case, non-producers will continue to produce at a minimum level once they realize their needs are met without exerting extra effort.

The productive ones will decrease their production, and those who get their needs met free and easily will opportunistically slow down their production. The latter does not want the state officials or anyone to know that they can do more; because more will be expected of them. They are not interested in working harder as long as they can get what they need otherwise. Besides, they know the extra work will only go to someone else who is a non-producer. In either situation, there are no incentives to work harder.

The overall production in society will decrease, and less productivity means fewer needs are met in general. The spiral of non-production continues downward until production is at a minimum. Society will suffer in poverty and desolation, with no one producing very much.

The communists do not believe in the concept *"from each according to his ability to each according to his accomplishments,"* as the marketplace dictates. To each according to his merits and achievements, or private charity (a social safety net established by our Creator) from others when in need is out of the question. Communists do not believe that one should reap the benefits of all of his labor. They advocate that one should reap the benefits of some of his labor, and some should go to someone else according to their choice.

> ***"When you reward nonproduction you get nonproduction. When you penalize production you get nonproduction"***
>
> *L. Ron Hubbard*

Also, communists believe in dialectics materialism. Dialectics materialism, according to Marx, is when there are two opposing forces (thesis and antithesis) colliding with one another, and they produce a third (synthesis). The new synthesis turns into another thesis that another antithesis will oppose. The conflict between the opposing forces will produce another synthesis. The process will continually repeat itself, resulting in continuous progress until a utopian communists society exists.

The synthesis, according to communists, is supposed to always represent historical human advancement or improvement. However, things don't always turn out that way in the real world. In life, change is the only constant. Growth and progress are not guaranteed; success and happiness are not, nor are peace and love. Things can turn out to be positive or negative, up or down, evolved or devolved.

Under dialectic materialism, if socialism and communism become the new synthesis, they will cause a reversal of human progress. Contrary to communists' assertions, socialism and communism will cause destruction, poverty, misery, and enslavement to humanity. Based on human nature and economic law, socialism and communism will undoubtedly usher the masses into another dark age that could last for generations. Another opposing force (a new antithesis) will have to be to bring about a new synthesis. The new synthesis must include free-market economics, limited government, personal responsibility, and God-consciousness. This new synthesis will put human progress back on track and bring about freedom, prosperity, and the fulfillment of God's purpose for man. The results will be peace, love, and happiness for the masses.

Many times in the history of humanity, instead of progression, digression will take place. And the duration of time is indefinite. It may range from short-term to long-term; maybe decades, centuries, millenniums, etc. Logical and reasonable people strive for what is right in theory and practice for what is accurate and just, and they pray and hope for the best.

Another concept advocated in communism is *"the withering away of the state."* If there is no state, there is no government and no law. Subsequently, pure communism leads to anarchy – total unplanned chaos! When no government results from the 'withering away' process, then all that is left is anarchy.

Communists do not believe in the principle of parliamentary or legislative government. They believe only in a dictatorship of the proletariat, even though it never gets pass the phase where some individual or small group is not the dictator.

Communists advocate violent revolution (killing innocent people and destroying property), and *"the end justifies the means."* However, the end pre-exists in the means. ***"Evil means lead to an evil end.... evil can never beget good....there is no such thing as short-range evils adding up to long-range good, and vice versa."*** Ralph Waldo Emerson stated that ***"cause and effect, means and ends, seed and fruit, cannot be severed; for the effect already blooms in the cause, the end pre-exists in the means, the fruit in the seed."*** In other words, cause and effect cannot be separated.

Communists do have a second strategy besides violent revolution to bring about their aim. Instead of revolutionary means, they use an evolutionary strategy. The Fabian Socialists developed this simple strategy. They work within the host country like parasites and leeches, using the democratic process to further their goal of bringing about communism. This is how the ten planks of the Communist Manifesto come into play.

They gradually implement the planks in a free market economy until it gets weaker and weaker, and people become dependent on the new socialistic institutions and programs. Using this strategy, they disguise themselves and their programs and never call them communistic or socialistic. This is done to keep the people duped and unaware of their hidden agenda. These undercover socialists never openly admit that they are socialists or communists themselves. They are wolves in sheep's clothing. They claim to want to help the people but only want control and power over them.

Communists believe that religion is the ***"opiate of the masses."*** They teach that the belief in God and religious practices should be abolished. Submission to the Creator is not allowed because, to communists, it conflicts with total submission to the state. And they want people to submit only to the state, or their system simply will not work.

On the contrary, religious people believe that there is no higher authority than the Creator, and they submit to Him first. This belief and behavior conflict directly with communism. When people submit to the Creator as the overriding authority in their lives, the communists lose control over them.

Communists do not want this type of competition. For their system to work, they need people to worship the state, not the Creator. Therefore, the state takes priority regarding worshiping the Creator or the 'state' under communist rule. During the brief history of communism, tens of millions of people have been killed and suffered because of their faith in the Creator.

Communists want to abolish all mediums of exchange (money) and establish a 'cashless society.' Communists advocate a 'cashless society' to stop private trading and exchanges without government awareness and approval. According to them, all private property must be abolished. They reason that if private property is not abolished, people could always find a way to exchange goods and services outside the supervision or authority of the state. And the goods and services being exchanged will constitute the 'mediums of exchange.' But communists do not want people to have freedom! This will give the people freedom and independence.

When people are allowed to own private property, they also maintain their independence and freedom. They will produce goods and services and exchange them for those produced by others without the state's control or even knowledge of the transactions. However, communists need *total* control of production, consumption, distribution, and redistribution, or their system will not work. The communist system will break down if the masses own private property, which they could use as *'mediums of exchange'* in the marketplace.

To do away with private property is to do away with freedom and independence. People will find themselves totally enslaved by the state. Without the state's approval, they will be unable to do anything, say anything, learn, work, play, vacation, travel, buy or sell, etc. They won't be able to marry and have as many kids as they desire without state approval. For the state to control the population, it will implement strong birth control measures, provide taxpayer-funded abortions, starve people to death, or start phony wars.

Communists also want to abolish the traditional family structure. Years ago, mothers stayed home, cooked, washed, cleaned, mended, made clothes and garments, grew gardens, prepared pickles, jams, and other preservatives, made candles, etc. As time passed, mothers stopped producing these items individually in the home.

Today, mothers have generally become a part of a workforce that produces these same items in factories and plants outside the home. They take the 'money' they earn and buy these same items in the marketplace. Nevertheless, wives and mothers continue to cook, wash, clean, and perform household duties. According to communists, these activities fall in the category of non-productive work. As far as the communists are concerned, this is too burdensome for women.

The communists believe it is a societal responsibility to free women from traditional house chores. Communists advocate that the state take responsibility for all the duties that normally fall on the traditional family. According to them, the state should establish communal kitchens and dining rooms for families. This way, working mothers will not have to cook for their families. What can be expected is that food from communal kitchens tastes inferior to home-cooked meals and that mothers will lose their traditional cooking skills.

Communists believe that society or the state should raise the children, feed and clothe them, and counsel and instructions for their intellectual development. Of course, religion will be excluded from their instructions if and when they get enough power and control. Most of this will be done through public education and social welfare agencies.

The state, according to communists, should also resort to regulating family planning, birth control or limit outright the number of children that can be born per family. This is an assault on the family and a part of the communist's plan to destroy it.

In America, this was the life work of Margaret Sanger. She is the founder of Planned Parenthood. She was an atheist, a socialist, and a racist. She led the *"Negro Project"* which targeted black women for birth control and later abortions. Her sole purpose and mission behind her work are summed up in one quote when she said, *"Colored people are like human weeds and are to be exterminated."*

Margaret Sanger won the support of black intellectuals such as W.E.B. Dubois and other so-called "Talented Tenth." Dubois, a leading influence over black Americans in the socialist/communist movement himself, stated: ***"The mass of ignorant Negroes still breed carelessly and disastrously, so that the increase among Negroes, even more than the increase among whites, is from that portion of the population least intelligent and fit, and least able to rear their children properly."***

Some estimate that as a result of this movement and her influence and the influence of men like Dubois, tens of millions of babies have been aborted, and as 'planned,' a larger percentage of them have been black babies. Taxpayers (whether they agreed or not with the movement) have been forced to participate in the funding of these abortions. Taxpayers today are still forced to pay for abortions because of them being financed or subsidized by the government.

Some undercover communists and their sympathizers advocate gay marriages as a strategy to weaken traditional marriages and the institution of the family. They promote it as natural and normal for a man to marry a man and a woman to marry a woman. As a consequence, there is no reproduction or perpetuation of the traditional family unit.

The workers must not forget that they must pay to finance these state enterprises, projects, and programs.

Under communism, no private educational system exists, only nationalized 'public' education. Only the elite can send their kids to private institutions which they classify as special public or state institutions. Education for the masses is standardized, centralized, and controlled. Everyone in the nation is indoctrinated (educated) in the same manner regarding religion, history, politics, and economics.

In fact, in many communist countries, it is difficult to find schools of business and schools of theology. No one or only a very few receive degrees in these subjects. And there is a minimum of professional businessmen and theologians. People are taught *only* what the rulers of the state want them to know. They are miseducated and taught falsehood, resulting in ignorance and confusion.

In a communistic system absent free-market forces, economic calculations are impossible. To determine costs, prices, rents, wages, etc., communists must go outside their economic domain to observe or imitate pricing in a 'free market' economic system. The otherwise fair and just economic calculation could not exist. All pricing, rents, wages, etc., would have to be established by politicians and bureaucratic committees. This is impossible when considering all the millions of diverse items requiring individual pricing based on time, place, and circumstances.

Other names and labels used for communism are socialism, fascism, Nazism, protectionism (against competition from monopolies, labor, special interest groups, industries, agriculture, etc.), interventionism, state capitalism, state planning, communal economics, cooperative economics, collective economics, and as euphemism macroeconomics.

Under communism, there is a small, rich class, a small middle class, and a very large poor class. There is little upward mobility from the poorer class to the middle class, nor from the middle class to the rich class.

> *"Everyone wants to live at the expense of the State. They forget that the state lives at the expense of everyone."*
>
> Frederic Bastiat, "The Law

*"Freedom is the uninterrupted interchange of ideas
and goods and services among individuals who worship
neither themselves nor one another. Freedom flows in the
absence of "big shots"; freedom springs from humility."*

Leonard E. Read Founder of FEE

# *The Freedom Formula*

*Limited Government + Free Enterprise economics + Personal Responsibility + God Consciousness = Freedom!*

# *The Freedom Formula*
# *Long Version*

*Limited Government (Constitutional Republic) + Free Enterprise Economics (private property, wealth medium of exchange, tax on natural resources and not on improvements income) + Personal Responsibility + God Consciousness (including charity) = Freedom!*

*"What is essential to the idea of a slave? We primarily think of him as one who is owned by another. That which fundamentally distinguishes the slave is that he labors under coercion to satisfy another's desires. ...." What... leads us to qualify our conception of the slavery as more or less severe? Evidently the greater or smaller extent to which effort is compulsorily expended for the benefit of another instead of for self-benefit."*

Herbert Spencer

# *The Slavery Formula*

*Statism + (Socialism, Communism) + Irresponsibility*
*+ Atheism = Slavery, Poverty, and Death!*

# *The Slavery Formula*
# *Long Version*

*Statism (Totalitarian Dictatorial Government, Monarchy,*
*Oligarchy, Democracy, Anarchy) + (Feudalism, Mercantilism,*
*Fascism, Nazism, Socialism, Communism, Mixed Economy) +*
*no personal responsibility + Atheism = Slavery, Poverty, Death!*

*To avoid "Big Business" (Profit or Non-Profit) undervaluing the voting rights of the people and usurping their power to control their own government, no corporation, foundation, union, or any other organization should be allowed to contribute "money" to any political party or political campaign. Only qualified individual voting citizens should be allowed to do so. Organizations do not vote; only individuals (real people) do. Therefore, only those who actually vote should support and contribute to political parties or political campaigns.*

*Suppose a corporation, foundation, union, or any other organization, favors a political party or thinks that a political campaign is worthy of donations. In that case, it can suggest to its members, without force or coercion, to contribute "monies." However, that is as far as it should legally be allowed to go. This will go a long way towards campaign reform. It will make it harder for politicians to exchange (sell) laws and legislation for big corporate "money."*

*It is similar to a religious establishment that does not contribute money to a particular political party or political campaign, but its leadership may mention to members its preference; after that, each member will make his or her own decision.*

*Taxes are paid for benefits received from the government, not for voting purposes. A person should be able to vote in some cases (not all) whether they pay taxes or not. There should be no tax right-off for any political "monetary" contributions by anyone, even in the form of charity, gifts, or any other name.*

***THE 13<sup>TH</sup> AMENDMENT FREEDOM WEEK MANUAL*** explains the difference between independence and freedom. It recognizes that many countries throughout the world celebrate their independence, but few celebrate freedom, including America. That is because few countries have both independence and freedom at the same time. It is possible for a country to have both independence and freedom simultaneously, or independence but not freedom, or neither independence nor freedom. In America, we celebrate Independence Day each year, but we have no occasion to celebrate 'freedom.' The *13<sup>th</sup> Amendment Freedom Week Movement* is designed to fill that void.

The 13<sup>th</sup> Amendment to the U.S. Constitution is the cornerstone of this manual. It is the foundation upon which all other rights, privileges, and responsibilities belonging to Black Americans in this country were built. ***The 13<sup>th</sup> Amendment Freedom Week Manual*** is written to provide an annual celebration week during the week of December 6<sup>th</sup> that educates as well as celebrates the beginning of freedom for ALL (not just some) American citizens.

This manual focuses on the ANTI-slavery movement in America, starting with the Quakers and Founding Fathers, and includes the courageous actions of the slaves and freed slaves themselves. It is hoped that it will give proper respect and honor to the brave souls who, with God's help, unleashed overwhelming powerful forces to break the chains of bondage for four million slaves and their descendants.

The manual is the foundation for the *13th Amendment Freedom Week Movement* and seeks to establish an annual weeklong celebration featuring something new to learn each day. It provides a consolidated and coherent system of knowledge that leads to a better understanding of the principles of freedom. It explains what freedom means and the difference between national independence and individual freedoms. The manual outlines a seven-day freedom celebration:

1. On Day One, the manual's focus is on outstanding abolitionists.

2. Day Two highlights the basic "forms" of government that may or may not contribute to freedom, justice, and equal opportunity.

3. On Day Three, the manual highlights various economic systems that may or may not contribute to freedom, justice, and equal opportunity.

4. On Day Four, the manual provides a list of historical documents that have contributed to freedom in America.

5. On Day Five, an awards luncheon or dinner takes place, and an exercise or special project in genealogical research is encouraged.

6. Day Six is Jubilee Day. It involves festivities, entertainment, and games are encouraged.

7. On Day Seven, "Guiding Principles for Reflection and Contemplation" are discussed. And on this day, participants can go to their respective places of worship and give thanks for the freedoms we have here in America.

***The 13th Amendment Freedom Week Manual*** features and highlights the 13th, 14th, and 15th Amendments and is unique in that it also lists the members of the 38th Congress, the 39th Congress, and the 40th Congress who voted for or against these Amendments, respectfully. The manual has in the appendices a list of historical documents, for research purposes, that impacted the freedom movement in America.

Freedom is essential regardless of one's race, religion, or creed!

# The Free Market Manifesto!

The *"Free Market Manifesto"* presents a counterrevolutionary struggle against all unnatural maladjustments that lead to special privileges, injustices, and corruption. Its goal is to restore freedom and prosperity to mankind. It highlights twenty Economic Bill of Rights that, if implemented, will stop the spread of Socialism/Communism in any country and will transform a Socialist's /Communist's nations into a free market economy with limited government and individual freedom and improve the standard of living for all its inhabitants. It will establish freedom, justice, and equal opportunity for all - Peace, Happiness, and Prosperity!

# *The 13ᵗʰ Amendment Freedom Week*

The ratification of the 13th Amendment to the U.S. Constitution was completed on December 6, 1865, by the legislative bodies representing 27 out of 36 states. It was this amendment that legally and constitutionally outlawed slavery…for all law-abiding citizens… in America forever. It invalidated the 3/5th Clause, voided Article IV Section 2 of the U.S. Constitution, and ended slavery in Kentucky, Delaware, West Virginia, and New Jersey. It made it impossible for the slave trade to be reinstated. It also stopped the possibility of the institution of future white indentured servants or of indentured servants of African, Asian, Native American, Chinese descent, etc.

December 6, 1865, is a day and a time in history that not enough Americans understand or remember. Commemoration of this day in American history should be taught and perpetuated by all Americans- especially the descendants of ex-slaves. Most of these descendants will see their true beginnings as free human beings, with great promise, at this critical time in the history of America.

December 6, 1865, should also be relevant for all Americans because it reflected the aspirations and foresight of the founders of this great country. During the 1787 Continental Convention, these visionary men instituted the Northwestern Ordinance and vowed to end the slave trade. They later incorporated the end of the slave trade in the U.S. Constitution: Article 1, section 9, clause 1. The official end of slavery in the United States, the author believes, was just an inevitability of their honorable intentions.

With the '13th Amendment Freedom Week Celebration', we can revisit this history and acknowledge the great men and women who sacrificed their lives and fortunes for the high principles that all men should be free and that another should own no man, woman, or child. This manual is an opportunity to review essential documents of American history and rediscover the tremendous impact they had in shaping America's past, present, and inevitable future. Although many of the individual abolitionists and the institutions they established lived beyond the 19th Century, the individuals, the events, legislations, and documents cited in this manual will conclude at the beginning of the Twentieth Century.

The '13th Amendment Freedom Week Celebration' will commemorate the ratification of the 13th Amendment. It will start on the first Monday of the week in which the 6th of December falls and will continue for seven days. In case there is a conflict in time with other holidays or historical events, The '13th Amendment Freedom Week' should take place as close to the 6th of December as possible.

This 'Freedom Week' falls within the school year. This program is set up to have extraordinary educational benefits for school-age children, beginning at pre-kindergarten and continuing through high school. This weeklong celebration will also have tremendous value for adults of all ages who take pride in America's antislavery/ freedom movement. This seven-day span will be a constant reminder of the achievements of the great men and women who contributed to freedom. It will provide a foundation for the continuance of freedom in America through insight and knowledge of the forms of government and the types of economic systems.

*"Every man, however obscure, however removed from the general recognition, is one of a group of men impressible for good, and impressible for evil, and it is in the nature of things that he cannot really improve himself without in some degree improving other men."*

*by Charles Dickens*

Kariem Abdul Haqq lives in North St. Louis County with his faithful and loving wife Marilyn and his beloved son Idris. He obtained a B.S. Degree in Economics from Missouri University – St. Louis (1980) and a Dual Master's Degree in Finance and International Business from Webster University (1989).

He has had a passion for the study of free market economics for a number of years. It started with a search for economical solutions for the problems confronting black people in particular and the world in general. He studied socialism at first, but he soon realized that it demonstrated a lack of objectivity, sincerity, and integrity to study just one perspective. So Kariem Abdul Haqq started studying free market economics, and that is when answers started coming.

Understanding how the economic and material world works was like taking off dark sunglasses, and everything seemed so much clearer. He came to the conclusion that the proper knowledge and application of good economic theory can eliminate poverty, eliminate moral decline, lessen racism, reduce crime, prevent wars, and establish peace and justice. His objectives have been to seek truth wherever it is found and advocate freedom, justice, and equal opportunity for all. He believes in studying the past, living the present, and planning for the future. His motto is: ***"great minds discuss ideas, average minds discuss events, and small minds discuss people."***

Kariem A. Haqq has written another book entitled <u>The 13<sup>th</sup> Amendment Freedom Week Manual</u>. This manual focuses on the ANTI-slavery movement in America, starting with the Quakers and the Founding Fathers. It ends with the Abolitionist Movement and the Reconstruction Era. It is hoped that it will give proper respect and honor to the brave souls who, with our Creators' help, unleashed overwhelming powerful forces to break the chains of bondage for four million slaves and their descendants.

Kariem A. Haqq is an author and the founder of the 13<sup>th</sup> Amendment Freedom Week Movement. It is based upon the author's monumental book. This Movement is to promote a celebration week that educates and celebrates the beginning of freedom for ALL (and not just some) American citizens. The 13<sup>th</sup> Amendment marks the first time in American history that ALL law-abiding Americans were legally freed.

*"That man thinks he knows everything, whereas*
*he knows nothing. I, on the other hand, know*
*nothing, but I know I know nothing."*

*Socrates*